Alarms & Excursions

Michael Frayn was born in 1933 in the suburbs of London. He began his career as a reporter on the *Guardian*, and became a columnist, first for the *Guardian*, then for the *Observer*. A selection of his columns, first published in four volumes, appeared as *The Original Michael Frayn*, and a collection of recent *Guardian* articles was published in 1995 under the title *Speak After the Beep*. He has written eight novels: *The Tin Men*, *The Russian Interpreter*, *Towards the End of the Morning*, *A Very Private Life*, *Sweet Dreams*, *The Trick of It*, *A Landing on the Sun* and *Now You Know*, together with a volume of philosophy, *Constructions*. He has also written screenplays for the cinema and TV: *Clockwise*, *First and Last* and *Remember Me?* as well as numerous stage plays including: *Alphabetical Order*, *Donkeys' Years*, *Clouds*, *Make and Break*, *Noises Off*, *Benefactors*, *Look Look*, *Here*, *Now You Know* and *Copenhagen*. He has translated Chekhov's last four plays, dramatised a selection of his one-act plays and short stories under the title of *The Sneeze* and adapted his first, untitled play, as *Wild Honey*. He has also translated one modern Russian play – Yuri Trifonov's *Exchange*.

Alarms & Excursions

more plays than one

Michael Frayn

Methuen Drama

Published by Methuen Drama

ISBN 0 413 73280 0

A CIP catalogue record for this book is available at the British Library

Typeset by Deltatype Ltd, Birkenhead, Merseyside
Transferred to digital printing 2003

Alarms & Excursions

Alarms & Excursions was first performed at the Yvonne Arnaud Theatre, Guildford, on 15 July 1998. The cast was as follows:

Actor A	Nicky Henson
Actress B	Felicity Kendal
Actor C	Robert Bathurst
Actress D	Josie Lawrence

Directed by Michael Blakemore
Produced by Michael Codron and Lee Dean
Designed by Lez Brotherston
Lighting by Paul Pyant
Music by Terry Davies
Sound by John A. Leonard

Characters

Act One

Alarms: Nicholas
John
Jocasta
Nancy

Doubles: Miles
Melanie
Laurence
Lynn

Act Two

Leavings Nicholas
Nancy
Jocasta
John

Look Away Now Aptly
Bloss
Charr
Voice of Stewardess

Heart to Heart Clifford
Chairmian
Peter

Glassnost The Right Honourable the Baroness Armament KO
GBH RSVP

Toasters Spott
Much
Candle
Voice of Speaker

Immobiles Dietrich
Chris
Nikki
Mother

The plays are to be performed by a team of two actors and two actresses:

Actor A and **Actress B**, both in their mid-forties
Actor C and **Actress D**, both in their mid-thirties

The likely distribution of parts would be:

Act One

	Actor A	**Actress B**	**Actor C**	**Actress D**
Alarms	John	Jocasta	Nicholas	Nancy
Doubles	Laurence	Lynn	Miles	Melanie

Act Two

	Actor A	**Actress B**	**Actor C**	**Actress D**
Leavings	John	Jocasta	Nicholas	Nancy
Look Away Now	Aptly	Charr	Bloss	Stewardess
Heart to Heart	Peter	--	Clifford	Charmian
Glassnost	Voice over PA	Lady Armament	--	--
Toasters	Speaker	Spott	Much	Candle
Immobiles	Chris	Mother	Dietrich	Nikki

Act One

Alarms

A table and four chairs. A phone, an answering machine. Three entrances: right, left and centre.

John, **Jocasta**, **Nicholas** *and* **Nancy**.

Nicholas   Just us?

John   Just you.

Jocasta   Is that all right?

Nancy   Wonderful.

Nicholas   Perfect.

John   We thought we'd simply flop down exhausted in our braces.

Jocasta   Have a nice quiet evening together.

John   Four old chums, grown bent and grey together over the years. Four weary fellow-travellers on the road of life, taking shelter for an hour or two from the night and storm.

Jocasta   Something very simple in the oven.

Nancy   Smells heavenly.

John   The odd bottle of wine.

He fetches one.

Nicholas   More and more like heaven.

Jocasta   Just have a look at the oven . . .

She goes out right.

John   Just open the wine . . .

He fetches an ingenious new corkscrew, and sets to work with it.

Then we can all ...

Nicholas   Flop down.

Nancy   Exhausted.

John   In our braces.

Nicholas   Where?

John   What?

Nicholas   Where do you want us to flop down?

John   Anywhere. On the floor. Under the sideboard. On a chair ... On a chair! Why not?

Nicholas   On a chair!

Nancy   Brilliant.

Nicholas   Any chair?

John   Absolutely any chair that takes your fancy.

Nicholas   The man's a prince.

Jocasta *enters right.*

Jocasta   You found somewhere to park?

Nicholas   Right outside.

Nancy   For once!

John   An augury, perhaps.

Nicholas   This is going to be one of the great evenings.

John   I'll just get the wine open ...

He struggles with the corkscrew.

Then we'll simply sit and ... I don't know ...

Chink.

Jocasta   Whatever one does when one gets the chance at last.

Nancy   What *does* one do, as a matter of fact?

Nicholas   So long since it happened.

Chink.

Jocasta Talk, perhaps?

Nancy Talk, yes! Talk, talk, talk!

Jocasta I remember talk.

Nicholas Get the wine open, possibly.

John Get the wine open, certainly.

He renews his efforts with the corkscrew.

Nicholas Or not even talk. Sit here in silence, why not?

Chink.

Nancy Relax. Be.

Nicholas Sip our wine.

John *withdraws his fingers sharply from the corkscrew.*

Nicholas New toy?

John The point is you don't have to do all that heaving and cursing. You just quite simply . . . No, hold on . . . Or possibly . . .

Nicholas Don't you put the . . . And then . . . ?

John I've got it, I've got it . . .

Nicholas No.

John Or . . .

Nicholas Try . . .

John Where are the instructions?

Jocasta I put them in the drawer.

John In the drawer?

Jocasta With all the other instructions.

Exit **Jocasta** *right.*

Nicholas Give it to me.

John It's all right.

Nicholas   Let me have a go!

John   No, if I can just . . .

Chink.

What?

Nicholas   What?

John   You made a little noise.

Nicholas   No?

John   It wasn't you?

Nicholas   What sort of noise?

John   Sort of . . . chink.

Chink.

There!

Nicholas   I thought that was you.

John   Me? Going chink?

Enter **Jocasta** *right, with the instructions.*

Jocasta   The instructions for everything – in the drawer.

Nicholas   Did you hear it?

Jocasta   Did I hear what?

John   Chink.

Jocasta   Chink?

Nancy   Chink.

Jocasta   What do you mean, chink?

Chink.

Nancy   There!

Jocasta   What is it?

John   That's what we want to know.

Nicholas   Something in the house.

Nancy   Some electronic thing.

Nicholas   The phone.

John   The phone? Phones don't go . . .

Chink.

Nicholas   Listen!

John   I've never heard a phone go chink!

Nancy   But you've got this special system.

Nicholas   This wonderful system.

Nancy   That sends calls all over the house.

John   Yes, but it doesn't go . . .

Chink.

It *is* you!

Nicholas   It is *not* me!

John   Something in your pocket.

Jocasta   A pager, maybe.

Nicholas   I haven't got a pager.

Nancy   You've got your . . .

Nicholas   What?

Nancy   . . . little whatsit thing.

Nicholas   What – this?

Nancy   No . . .

Nicholas   This?

John   Pocketsful of the stuff.

Nancy   That's electronic.

Nicholas   Yes, but it doesn't go . . .

Chink.

Nancy   What – me?

Jocasta   Something in your bag.

Nancy   Don't be silly.

Nicholas   Let's have a look.

Nancy   No!

Nicholas   *I* got everything out of *my* pockets.

Nancy   I don't keep things like that in my bag! There's nothing in there that could possibly go . . .

Chink.

Nicholas   It's the opening thing.

John   The opening thing?

Nicholas   Your new bottle-opening thing.

John   Going chink?

Nicholas   To remind you.

John   To do what?

Nicholas   To open the wine.

Jocasta   Yes. Come on.

Chink, chink.

Nicholas   There! Twice! Chink chink! It's getting desperate!

Jocasta   No, but as soon as you touched it!

Nancy   Try not touching it!

Nicholas   Put it down!

Nancy   Listen . . . !

Nicholas   Silence.

Nancy   Wait . . . wait . . .

Nicholas   You see?

Nancy   If you don't touch it it doesn't go . . .

Chink.

Nicholas   It's the oven.

Jocasta   The oven?

Nancy   You said you'd got something in the oven.

Jocasta   The oven doesn't go . . .

Chink.

Nancy   No, but the timer thing.

Jocasta   The timer thing? The timer thing goes . . .

Buzz.

Excuse me . . .

She goes off right.

Nancy   *Something* in the kitchen, though. The microwave.

Nicholas   Or the food-processor.

Nancy   The coffee-maker.

Nicholas   The coffee-grinder.

The buzzing stops.

Nancy   The toaster.

Jocasta   The toaster?

John   How can a toaster go . . . ?

Chink. Enter **Jocasta** *right.*

Jocasta   Anyway, let's all just forget about it.

John   But it's plainly trying to tell us something.

Jocasta   But if we don't know what it is . . .

Nicholas   It could be something important.

Jocasta   It can't be *that* important!

John   But it's plainly *meaningful!*

Silence.

Nancy   Listen!

Nicholas   What?

Nancy   It's stopped.

Silence.

Jocasta   Right. It's stopped. Where were we? What were talking about?

Nancy   The chink.

Jocasta   Before that.

Nicholas   I can't remember.

Jocasta   Open the wine, at least.

John   I'm trying to.

Buzz.

Jocasta   Sorry.

Jocasta *goes off right.*

Nancy   Timer?

Jocasta (*off*)   Sometimes you turn it off, and two minutes later . . .

Nicholas   It's rather nice, the buzz.

Nancy   Like bees.

John   Soporific.

Nancy   Summer afternoon.

Nicholas   Glass of wine in front of you . . .

John   Turn it *off!*

Jocasta (*off*)   I'm trying to!

Buzzing stops. **Jocasta** *returns.*

Jocasta   I keep meaning to get the man. Sorry.

Nicholas   And at least we haven't got the . . .

Chink.

Nancy   It's some sort of creature.

Nicholas   Creature?

Nancy   A cricket. A frog. Some sort of tropical frog. Perhaps it was someone's pet, and it escaped. Now it's trapped somewhere.

Chink.

It's getting desperate.

Chink.

It's in the ceiling . . .

They watch. Chink.

Jocasta   It's the smoke alarm.

Nancy   Oh my God.

Nicholas   The house is on fire.

John   Except it isn't.

Nancy   Is it?

Nicholas   The machine says it is!

John   Well, it's wrong.

Nicholas   A smoke alarm must know more about smoke than you do!

John   It's lying.

Nicholas   That's a terrible accusation.

John   There is no smoke.

Nicholas   There must be smoke.

John   Look!

Nicholas   I don't need to look. I can hear.

Nancy   I can smell burning.

They all sniff. Buzz.

Nicholas   I can smell buzzing.

Jocasta   Sorry.

Exit **Jocasta** *right.*

Nicholas   It's not a smoke alarm. It's an alarm alarm.

The buzzing stops.

Listen . . . You see? No buzz, no . . .

Chink.

Nancy   Perhaps it needs a new battery.

Nicholas   Perhaps we need the instructions.

Enter **Jocasta** *right carrying a drawer.*

Jocasta   In here somewhere.

She dumps the contents on the table.

Nicholas   These are all instructions? Instructions for gadgets? You have gadgets to fit all these instructions?

John   Of course not. We throw out the gadgets when they break down.

Jocasta   We never throw out the instructions.

John   The instructions don't break down.

Nicholas   Hair-curler . . . Eyebrow-trimmer . . . Toaster . . .

Jocasta   We don't need instructions for the toaster!

She puts the book aside.

John   We might.

He puts it back. Chink.

Nancy   Perhaps it's trying to tell us it needs a new battery.

Nicholas   Electric carving-knife ... You haven't got an electric carving-knife!

Jocasta   We threw the electric carving-knife out ten years ago!

She puts the book aside. **Nicholas** *puts it back.*

Nicholas   You never know. Christmas Day. In rushes the man from across the street, desperate. Turkey on the table, fifteen people to dinner, and the carving-knife is going chink.

John   Here we are – smoke alarm.

Jocasta   Right at the bottom. The house could have burnt down by now.

Nancy   I think it may just need ...

Nicholas   Yes, we heard you.

Nancy   ... a new battery.

Nicholas   Don't be silly. Things don't go ...

Chink.

... to tell you they need a new battery.

John *reads the instructions.*

John   It needs a new battery.

Nicholas   It needs a new battery. Obviously.

John   Just help me ... Thanks.

John *and* **Nicholas** *drag the table under the smoke alarm.* **John** *climbs on it.*

Jocasta   Have we got a new battery?

Nicholas   Of course you haven't. But if he takes out the old battery, at least it won't keep going ...

Chink. Buzz. Exit **Jocasta** *right. Phone. Enter* **Jocasta** *right.*

Nicholas   I'll get it ...

Exit **Jocasta** *right.*

(*Into phone.*) Hello ...? No, he's dealing with the chink ... The chink ... Yes – he's standing on the table. Can he ...? No, OK, hold on ... (*To* **John**.) Rather urgent.

Buzz stops.

John   Cordless.

Nancy   Where?

Enter **Jocasta** *right, holding cordless phone.*

Jocasta   Here ...

John   Thanks.

Nicholas   What do I do?

John   Press nine.

Nicholas (*presses*)   Nine.

Jocasta   Not nine!

John   Not nine!

Jocasta   You're always doing this!

John   I mean eight!

Jocasta   Nine's the living-room! It's gone into the living-room now!

She starts to exit centre.

John   You don't have to run after it! You can get it back, you can get it back!

Jocasta   You can get it back if you can remember what to press to get it back, but you can never remember what to press!

Buzz.

Oh, no!

Nancy   Living-room? I'll go, I'll go!

John   Sit down, sit down!

Nicholas   They didn't pay whatever it was for this wonderful system to have people go running all over the house like sheepdogs, rounding up stray calls.

John Just press ... what is it?

Chink.

Jocasta You're going to make a mess of it, whatever you do.

Exit **Jocasta** *right.*

Nancy It'll just be quicker for me to ...

Exit **Nancy** *centre.*

John Press Recall.

Nicholas (*presses*) Recall.

Enter **Jocasta** *right.*

Jocasta No! Not Recall!

John I mean Redial!

Nicholas (*presses*) Redial.

Jocasta Certainly not Redial! You'll never get it back now!

John It's that buzzer! I can't think with that buzzer going!

Chink. Enter **Nancy** *centre.*

Nancy It stopped just as I picked it up.

Jocasta It's ringing in the bedroom now.

Nancy Bedroom, right.

Jocasta It rings each extension in turn.

Nancy Which bedroom?

John Front.

Jocasta Back.

John Front first!

Jocasta Back first!

Exit **Nancy** *centre.*

John   It doesn't matter . . .

Nicholas   He sounded desperate.

John   . . . because it'll end up on the answering machine. We'll hear it on the answering machine . . .

Chink.

(*To* **Jocasta**.) Buzzer, buzzer! (*To* **Nicholas**.) We'll pick it up on the answering machine.

Jocasta   You can't pick it up on the answering machine! We're always trying to pick it up on the answering machine, and you can't!

John   You can if you do it from the downstairs bathroom.

Jocasta   No, from the study.

John   The downstairs bathroom!

Jocasta   The study!

Enter **Nancy** *centre.*

Nancy   It wasn't the front bedroom . . .

Jocasta   No, it was the back! *Now* it's the front!

John   No, *now* it's the upstairs bathroom! (*To* **Jocasta**.) Will you stop that *buzzing*? It's driving me mad!

Nancy   Upstairs bathroom?

Nicholas   My turn.

Exit **Jocasta** *right.*

(*To* **Nancy**.) You open the wine.

Chink.

John (*to smoke alarm*)   Oh, shut up!

Exit **Nicholas** *centre. Car alarm. Enter* **Nicholas** *centre.*

Nicholas   Not yours?

John   Or yours?

Nicholas   Oh, *no*, not again!

Exit **Nicholas** *left.*

John (*to* **Nancy**)   Open the wine. It sounds as if he might need a drink.

The buzzer stops. Enter **Jocasta** *right.*

Jocasta (*to* **Nancy**)   What are you doing?

Nancy   Opening the wine.

Jocasta   Not with that thing!

John   What do you mean, not with that thing!

Nancy   I'm not very good with gadgets.

John   It's *easier* with that thing!

Jocasta   I'll get you an ordinary one.

Exit **Jocsata** *right. Doorbell.*

Nancy   What's that?

John   Doorbell.

Enter **Jocasta** *right.*

Jocasta   Who on earth?

Nancy   I'll go.

John   *I'll* go! (*To* **Nancy**.) Wine, wine!

He gets down from the table and exits left.

Jocasta (*to* **Nancy**)   Wait! Corkscrew!

Exit **Jocasta** *right.*

Voice on answering machine   John, are you there or aren't you . . . ?

Enter **John** *left.*

John   Oh, God, it's got on the answering machine!

Voice   If I can't get hold of you I don't know what we're going to do.

John   Give me a number! Get off the line! I'll call you back!

Voice   John . . . ? I know you're there . . .

Enter **Jocasta** *right.*

Jocasta   Who *is* this?

John   I've no idea!

Voice   You could end up in court.

Jocasta   In court? What's happening?

John   I don't know!

Voice   It could cost you a lot of money . . . John . . . ?

Jocasta   Pick it up, pick it up!

John   Downstairs bathroom?

Exit **John** *centre.*

Jocasta (*calls after him*)   Study! Study!

Doorbell.

Nancy   The door . . .

Jocasta   *I'll* go!

Buzzer.

You do the buzzer. No, leave it, leave it.

Nancy   I'll do the wine.

Jocasta   No! Wait! Don't do anything!

Exit **Jocasta** *left. Enter* **John** *centre.*

John   I can't! It won't! Nothing happens!

Voice   John . . . ? John . . . ? Will you please pick up the phone . . . !

John (*to answering machine*)   I *have*! I've gone into the downstairs bathroom and picked it up, and it still doesn't work! (*To* **Nancy**.)

Not like that! You'll have your finger off!

Takes wine and gadget.

Voice   John! Please!

Enter **Nicholas** *and* **Jocasta** *left.*

Nicholas   Not mine.

John   Oh, good.

Voice   We're talking about several thousand pounds here . . .

John (*to answering machine*)   Give me a *number*! Get off the *line*!

Nicholas   What's all this?

John   I have not the faintest notion!

Car alarm.

Oh, these bloody people and their car alarms . . . And that buzzer!
I'll boot that buzzer into touch for a start!

Exit **John** *right.*

Jocasta   I'll do it!

Exit **Jocasta** *right.*

Nicholas   Blue Renault.

Enter **John** *right.*

John   Blue Renault?

Nicholas   Isn't that yours?

John   Oh *no*!

Exit **John** *left, followed by* **Nicholas**.

Nicholas   There's glass everywhere . . .

Enter **John** *left, followed by* **Nicholas**. *He hands the wine to* **Nancy**.

John   Hold this. Don't try to do it.

Nicholas   The stereo's gone . . .

Exit **John** *left, followed by* **Nicholas**.

Voice   Several *hundred* thousand pounds . . . !

*Enter **John** left.*

John *(stops)*   Several *hundred* . . . ? *(Calls.)* You did say *downstairs*? You did say *downstairs* bathroom?

Jocasta *(off)*   What?

Nancy   No, I think she said . . .

John   Upstairs? She said upstairs? You pick it up from the *upstairs* bathroom?

Nancy   Well, I think she said . . .

*Exit **John** centre.*

. . . the study.

*Enter **Jocasta** right.*

Jocasta   The buzzer's completely jammed . . . ! What is it? What's he want?

Nancy   He said was it the upstairs bathroom?

Jocasta   Study! Study!

Nancy   I'll tell him.

Jocasta   *I'll* tell him.

*The car alarm stops. Exit **Jocasta** centre.*

Nancy   I'll just open the . . .

Nancy *attempts to open the bottle, screams and drops it. Enter **Jocasta** centre.*

Jocasta   What, what?

Nancy   I'm so sorry. I think I've . . .

Jocasta   Oh, no!

*Enter **Nicholas** left.*

Nicholas   What in heaven's name . . . ?

Jocasta   Her finger!

Nicholas   You know you can't do anything mechanical!

Jocasta   Is there an artery in your finger?

Nancy   I'm fine, I'm fine.

Nicholas   Hold it up in the air ... You're getting blood over everything!

Jocasta   Tourniquet ...

Nicholas   Tea cloth!

Nancy   Don't fuss, I'm fine.

Nicholas   No, but it's going everywhere! Newspaper! I'm so sorry about this.

Jocasta   Casualty! Get her to casualty!

Nancy   I just feel a bit faint ...

Jocasta   Casualty! Casualty!

Jocasta *and* **Nicholas** *hustle* **Nancy** *away left.*

Nicholas   I'm so sorry.

Nancy   I think I *did* get it open. I think it's pouring over the carpet.

Jocasta (*calls*)   John! *John* ...! Leave that! Emergency!

Nicholas   *I'll* tell him! You get her into the car!

Exit **Nicholas** *centre.*

Jocasta (*calls after him*)   He's in the upstairs bathroom!

She rushes **Nancy** *off left.*

(*To* **Nancy**.) Keep calm! There's nothing to worry about!

Enter **John** *centre.*

John   I *knew* you couldn't do it from the upstairs bathroom! Where are you ...? Where is everybody?

Voice   Still here ... Still waiting ...

Enter **Jocasta** *and* **Nancy** *left.*

Jocasta   Door-keys! Haven't got my door-keys!

John   What in heaven's name . . . ?

Jocasta   Bleeding! Bottle! Finger! Casualty!

John   Oh, my God!

Jocasta   Car! Get her into the car!

John *rushes* **Nancy** *off left.*

Jocasta   Door-keys!

Exit **Jocasta** *right. Enter* **John** *and* **Nancy** *left.*

John   Car! Broken glass!

Enter **Jocasta** *right.*

Jocasta   Their car!

John   Their car.

Exit **John** *and* **Nancy** *left.*

Jocasta   What was I doing . . . ? Door-keys!

Exit **Jocasta** *right. Enter* **Nicholas** *centre.*

Nicholas   Not in the upstairs bathroom . . . You didn't say the *study*? You didn't say the *attic* . . . ?

Exit **Nicholas** *centre. Enter* **John** *and* **Nancy** *left.*

John   Door-keys! Haven't got the door-keys!

Nancy   I think I'm going to faint.

John   Car! Car! Get in the car!

Nancy *remains where she is, dazed. Enter* **Jocasta** *right.*

John   Door-keys!

Jocasta   Door-keys!

John   On the hook!

Exit **John** *right.*

Jocasta *(after* **John***)*   Not on the hook!

Nancy I'm so sorry . . .

Jocasta (*to* **Nancy**) In the car! (*After* **John.**) I've just looked!

Exit **Jocasta** *right.*

Nancy I don't think I can quite . . .

She sits down and puts her head between her knees.

The buzzer stops. Enter **John** *right, with a large cast-iron saucepan.*

John (*after* **Jocasta**) Not on the hook!

Enter **Jocasta** *right.*

Jocasta I *said* – not on the . . .

She sees the saucepan.

John Table.

Jocasta Saucepan?

John Buzzer. Fixed the buzzer. Table!

Jocasta Table?

John (*searches*) Door-keys! On the table . . . ! Under the table! Move the table!

He puts the saucepan down on the table and struggles to drag it back into its original position, where it conceals **Nancy**, *without noticing her.*

Doing the thing! With the door-keys! Put them down! Fell on the floor!

No sign of them there. Enter **Nicholas** *centre.*

Nicholas Not in the study.

John The door-keys?

Nicholas You.

John Me?

Nicholas Looking for you.

John I'm here.

Nicholas   Slight problem with the . . .

John   I know!

Nicholas   Where is she?

John   In the car!

Nicholas   In the car?

Jocasta (*to* **Nicholas**)   In the car!

Nicholas   In the car . . .

Exit **Nicholas** *left.*

Jocasta   Try the bedroom!

John   The bedroom?

Exit **John** *centre. Enter* **Nicholas** *left.*

Nicholas   The bedroom?

Jocasta (*calls after* **John**)   By the bed! On the bed!

Nicholas   On the *bed?*

Jocasta (*to* **John**)   *Under* the bed!

Nicholas (*to* **John**)   *Under* the bed?

Nicholas *goes towards the centre exit.*

Jocasta (*to* **Nicholas**)   The keys! Her? In the car!

Nicholas   In the car . . .

Exit **Nicholas** *left. Enter* **John** *centre, waving door-keys.*

John   By the phone!

Jocasta   In the car!

John   In the car! Burglar alarm!

Jocasta   Burglar alarm!

Exit **John** *and* **Jocasta** *left.*

Voice   Three years, John – *five* years . . . !

Four pips, as burglar alarm is set, followed by warbling tone.

Enter **John** *left.*

John   Five years?

Nicholas (*off*)   She's not in the car!

Enter **Nicholas** *left.*

Nicholas   Where is she?

Enter **Jocasta** *left.*

Jocasta   She's in the car!

Nicholas   She's not in the car!

John   Five years!

Jocasta   Alarm, alarm!

She bundles **John** *and* **Nicholas** *off left. Sound of front door slamming. Continuous tone from burglar alarm.*

Voice   Come on! You can't just sit there with your head in the sand!

Nancy *sits up groggily from behind the table.*

Nancy   Sorry. Just coming.

Jocasta (*off*)   Keys! Keys! Who's got the keys?

John (*off*)   I've got the keys!

Sound of front door opening. Continuous tone from burglar alarm turns to urgent interrupted warning tone. **Nancy** *subsides behind the table again. Enter* **Jocasta**, **Nicholas** *and* **John**, *left.*

Jocasta (*calls*)   Nancy!

John (*calls*)   Nancy!

Jocasta   I thought she was in the car!

Nicholas   I told you she wasn't in the car!

Jocasta (*calls*)   Nancy!

John   Alarm!

Jocasta   Alarm . . .

Exit **Jocasta** *left. Four pips as burglar alarm is disarmed.*

John (*calls*)   Nancy!

Exit **John** *right, searching.* **Nancy** *sits up again.*

Nancy   Sorry. I can't quite . . .

She disappears behind the table again.

Nicholas   What on earth . . . ?

Nicholas *drags the table out of the way. Enter* **Jocasta** *left.*

Jocasta   Where on earth . . . ?

Nicholas   Under the table!

Jocasta *and* **Nicholas** *rush* **Nancy** *off left. Four pips as burglar alarm is set, followed by warbling tone.*

Enter **John** *right.*

John   She was under the table?

Jocasta (*off*)   Lights!

John   Lights . . .

Exit **John** *right to switch off the kitchen lights. Enter* **Nicholas** *left.*

Nicholas   Lights . . .

He switches off lights by lefthand exit. Darkness. The slam of the front door. Continuous tone from burglar alarm.

Enter **John** *right, invisible in the darkness.*

John   Stop! Wait! I'm still inside!

Crash as he runs into the displaced table. The continuous tone from the burglar alarm finishes. Silence. Chink. Groan.

Voice   Come on, John, pull yourself together . . .

Doorbell. Knocker.

Jocasta (*off*)   John, open the door! I haven't any keys!

Nicholas (*off*)   The alarm's on!

Jocasta (*off*)   Keep absolutely still!

Nicholas (*off*)   Turn the alarm off!

Jocasta (*off*)   Don't move, or the alarm will . . .

Another groan. Something moves in the darkness. A high intermittent warning sound from the alarm.

(*Off.*)   I said, Don't move!

Nicholas (*off*)   Turn it off! Turn it off!

Jocasta (*off*)   You've got about fifteen seconds! Fourteen! Thirteen . . . !

A light comes on. **John** *is standing, with his hand on the switch and the saucepan on his head. The table is on its side.*

Nicholas (*off*)   Come on, come on!

Jocasta (*off*)   What are you doing?

Nicholas (*off*)   Do something!

Jocasta (*off*)   It's going to go off! It's going to go off!

Voice   No? Sit down, then, and I'll tell you what this is all about.

John *takes the saucepan off his head and subsides, still stunned, into a chair.*

Now, listen carefully . . .

He listens carefully. Doorbell. Door-knocker. Hammering on door with fists. Flapping of letter-box. Buzzer. Car alarm. Police siren. The burglar alarm goes off.

Curtain.

Doubles

Two standard small hotel double bedrooms, arranged so that they are mirror images of each other. Upstage in each room is the door to the corridor. Beside the doors are boxed-off shower/toilets, back-to-back against the party wall. Double beds, also back to back against the party wall. The party wall itself is irregularly cut away as it comes downstage, as in a sectional drawing, so that at the downstage end it is entirely notional, apart from the back-to-back frames of full-length mirrors. Along the opposite wall of each bedroom is the same array of standard equipment: TV; a fitted wall unit that includes luggage stand, hanging space and built-in desk; a mini-bar; an electric kettle; a trouser-press. Downstage each room has a balcony.

LEFTHAND ROOM

Darkness. Then the lights come up as the upstage door opens to reveal **Miles**. *He is carrying an overnight bag and other travel impedimenta. He stops uneasily.*

Miles This room . . .

Melanie *enters behind him, also carrying bags and coats.*

Melanie (*anxiously*) Is it all right?

Miles (*eerily*) There's something familiar about it . . .

Melanie It looks all right.

He dumps his bag on the bed.

Miles TV . . . Mini-bar . . . Have we somehow . . . gone back in time to the hotel we stayed in last night? Look – it's the same balcony! It's the same view over the hotel car-park!

RIGHTHAND ROOM

Darkness.

Melanie (*matter-of-fact*)   What about the bathroom?

She goes into it.

Miles   Yes! The bathroom's different. Last night it was here.

He indicates the lefthand wall by the window.

Is it the hotel we stayed in the the night *before* last? Or have we . . . strayed *forward* in time to the hotel we're going to be staying in tomorrow night?

She comes out of the bathroom.

Melanie   If it's *clean* – that's all I care about.

She starts to unpack.

Miles   We must write to the Good Hotel Guide. 'One satisfied couple were specially struck by the charming sense of *déjà-vu* about the complimentary tea bags and sterilised milk.'

Melanie   Aren't you going to unpack?

She lays out her stuff on the downstage side of the bed.

Miles   Actually this particular pattern of cigarette burns on the carpet we *haven't* seen before.

He reads a notice on the wall.

'For the safekeeping of personal possessions the management is entirely irresponsible.' That's new.

Melanie   I wish you wouldn't put your suitcase on the bed.

Miles   'Our esteemed guests are advised that chuckout time is noon.'

Melanie   You could press your trousers.

Miles   I could what?

Melanie   There's a trouser-press.

Miles   Good God, we haven't had a trouser-press before! I shall always think of this as the Place with the Trouser-press.

Melanie   Sit down. Read a book, or something.

She comes downstage and inspects herself in the full-length mirror, indicated notionally by its frame, between the bed and the window, on the notional party wall . . .

Miles   Read a book? All right.

He picks up the directory of hotel services.

'Why not relax over a pre-dinner cocktail in the intimate atmosphere of the Commodore's Cabin?'

Melanie   To yourself.

She goes on inspecting herself, dissatisfied, in the mirror. He watches her, then turns back to the directory.

Miles 'As you sip you can study the choice of specially selected local and international dishes in our celebrated Downtowner Dining-room and Groll.'

Melanie At least take your suitcase off the bed.

He moves it on to the floor beside the TV.

Miles When you think of them all, though. All the people who've been in this room before us. Unpacked their bags.

He opens his bag.

Packed them up again. Dropped their lighted cigarettes on the carpet. 365 couples a year. They come through the door. They look round. She checks the bathroom. He reads out the funny English. Together they discover the complimentary trouser-press . . .

Melanie I'm going to have a shower.

She retires into the bathroom. He sinks down on the bed, suddenly gloomy.

Miles And then you think – how many rooms are there in the hotel? 200? 300? So every night 300 doors are opening, and 300 couples are coming in, and looking round, and reading out about the chuckout time and the Groll, and discovering the trouser-press ... So that's 100,000 couples a year ... 10,000 hotels, all the same. A thousand million couples. Every couple having the same experiences ... All turning into the same couple, repeated a thousand million times ...

He gives up his attempt at unpacking, overcome with gloom.

The lights come up as the upstage door opens to reveal **Laurence**. *He is carrying an overnight bag and other travel impedimenta. He looks round the room.*

Laurence   Trouser-press.

He advances into the room, followed by **Lynn**, *also carrying bags and coats.*

Trouser-press, look.

Lynn   So I see.

Laurence   What?

Lynn   Nothing.

Laurence   Don't like it?

Lynn   Lovely.

Laurence   No different from the one last night.

Lynn   Or the night before.

Laurence   You liked them.

Lynn Did I?

Laurence It's only for one night.

Laurence Some sort of brown stuff spilt down the wall.

Laurence Well, that makes a change.

Lynn Very distinctive.

Laurence Come on! We'll be somewhere else tomorrow night.

Lynn I know. Somewhere like this.

Laurence Balcony. Nice view.

Lynn It's the hotel car-park.

Laurence It could be the gasworks.

Lynn You can keep an eye on the car.

Laurence Give it a rest.

Lynn That's all you worry about.

Laurence I know. Cup of tea?

Lynn No, thanks.

Laurence Kettle. All the doings.

Lynn I don't want one!

Laurence Mini-bar ... You want a drink?

Lynn   What's the bathroom like?

She looks into it. He goes on inspecting the equipment of the room.

Laurence   Biscuits ... biscuits ... more biscuits ...

Lynn *comes out of the bathroom.*

Lynn   It's sanitised for our personal protection.

Laurence   Good. No shortage of biscuits!

Lynn   We've got our own biscuits.

Laurence   Well, now we've got some spare ones.

He lays out his stuff on the upstage side of the bed.

I'll go this side, OK?

Lynn   What are you asking for?

Laurence   Go the other way round if you like. We're on holiday.

Lynn *(reads a notice on the wall)* 'Our esteemed guests are advised that chuckout time is noon.'

Laurence   Noon? Right.

Lynn   Chuckout time.

Laurence   Aren't you going to unpack?

Lynn   'For the safekeeping of personal possessions the management is entirely irresponsible.'

Laurence   Yes – don't go leaving your handbag in the room this time.

He unpacks. She picks up the directory of hotel services on the desk.

Lynn   'Why not relax over a pre-dinner cocktail in the intimate atmosphere of the Commodore's Cabin?'

Laurence   Have a drink here if you want one.

Lynn   'As you sip you can study the choice of specially selected local and international dishes in our celebrated Downtowner Dining-room and Groll.'

Laurence   Do you want a drink or don't you?

Lynn   I want a nice grolled steak. Medium rear. With chaps and poos.

Laurence   Don't go mad. You'll be up all night again.

He takes his trousers off.

Lynn   What – pressing your trousers?

Laurence   Why not? While we've got the chance?

He puts his trousers in the press. She watches him gloomily.

Lynn   Funny, when you think there was someone else taking off his trousers in here last night.

She comes downstage and looks at herself in the notional full-length mirror on the party wall between the bed and the window.

Someone else in that mirror. Looking back at themselves.

Laurence   Moaning away about everything.

Lynn   Someone else the night before that. Someone else tomorrow night. Someone on the other side of the wall . . .

She sinks down on to the bed, overcome by melancholy. He inspects his bare legs.

Laurence   Might as well have a crap, now I've got them off.

He goes into bathroom.

Miles (*calls*)   Shall I come and scrub your back . . . ?

Lynn (*calls*)   What?

Shall I come and work on various parts of you?

What are you mumbling about?

Melanie (*off*)   What?

Laurence (*off*)   What?

Miles   I said . . . Oh, never mind.

He turns on the TV. The screen faces upstage, but there is the sound of an announcer reading a news bulletin in Rewindese, the language a recording makes when it's run backwards. He watches gloomily for a few moments, then presses the remote, and the news is replaced by the sounds of a Rewindese love scene.

Enter **Melanie**, *in a dressing-gown, from the bathroom.*

Melanie   You're not going to leave your bag there?

He instantaneously switches back to the news. Pause. He becomes aware of her.

Miles   What?

Pause.

Melanie   What are you watching?

Miles   No idea.

Melanie   What's it about?

Miles   Shortfall in self-adhesive envelope production.

Lynn   I said . . . Oh, never mind.

She turns on the TV. The screen faces upstage, but there is the sound of an announcer reading a news bulletin in Rewindese, the language a recording makes when it's run backwards. She watches gloomily for a few moments, then presses the remote, and the news is replaced by the sounds of a Rewindese love scene.

Enter **Laurence**, *still trouserless, from the bathroom.*

Laurence   Changed my mind.

She instantaneously switches back to the news. Pause. She becomes aware of him.

Lynn   What?

Pause.

Laurence   What's all this, then?

Lynn   Search me.

Laurence   Where's the whatsit?

Melanie   Try the other channels.

She picks up the remote and presses the button. The sound of the love scene.

Oh dear.

She gazes at the screen, in spite of herself. So does he.

Miles   She's trying to tell him she reversed the car into a bollard.

She switches off.

Miles   Oh.

Melanie   Somebody's going to fall over that bag.

Miles   Me.

Melanie   Probably. It was you last night.

Miles   And the night before.

He puts his hand under her dressing-gown.

Melanie (*startled*)   What?

He picks up the remote and presses the button. The sound of the love scene.

Oh dear oh dear.

He gazes at the screens in spite of himself. So does she.

Lynn   She's trying to tell him something.

Laurence   We don't want to watch this kind of thing, do we?

He switches off.

Lynn   Oh.

She puts her hand on his bare knee.

Laurence (*baffled*)   What?

Lynn   Since you've got your trousers off already . . .

Miles   Another letter to the Good Hotel Guide. 'One guest complained about the shocking flimsiness of his partner's underwear.'

Laurence   They should be done by now.

Melanie (*pushes his hand away*)   I've had my shower.

She begins to get dressed. He inspects himself gloomily in the full-length mirror, turning his head this way and that.

He goes to inspect the trouser-press. She inspects herself gloomily in the full-length mirror, turning her head this way and that.

Melanie   Aren't you going to change?

Miles   I have. Out of all recognition.

Lynn   I don't look like that, do I?

I never used to look like that.

Melanie   I thought we were going to eat?

Miles   Do I exist as a continuous entity?

Melanie   You know what'll happen . . .

Miles   Close my eyes for a moment . . .

Laurence   We eating, or what?

Lynn   Do something to my face.

And when I open them . . .

She goes to fetch her handbag.

(*In alarm.*) ... I've vanished!

Melanie   They'll have stopped serving.

She returns and begins to make up her face in the mirror.

Miles (*depressed*)   No, I haven't.

He puts his face very close to the mirror, and contorts it as he examines it.

She puts her face very close to the mirror, and contorts it as she makes up.

Do *you* think I've changed?

But is that really me?

I still look like me if I put a bit of make-up on, don't I?

Or is that some complete stranger gazing back at me?

She holds up a pair of trousers to examine.

He holds up the pressed trousers.

Laurence   How about that?

Melanie   Got a bit crumpled.

He glances round.

She glances round.

Lynn   Wonderful.

Miles   Perfect.

He turns back to the mirror.

She turns back to the mirror.

I suppose I'm talking to myself.

I suppose I'm talking to myself. (*To her image.*) Hello!

(*To his image.*) Hello!

How are *you* today?

What's it like in there?

You're trying to say something.

I didn't quite catch what you said.

You always speak at exactly the same time as I do!

She joins him at the mirror, to inspect the effect of her trousers.

Melanie What do you think?

Miles I said – perfect.

Melanie Not *too* creased?
Miles Wonderful.

Come here.

He indicates their image in the mirror.
That's us.

What do you think?
Melanie What do I think?

Did you say something?

What was that?

The trouble is . . .

You always speak at exactly the same time as I do!

He joins her at the mirror, to inspect the effect of his trousers.

Laurence All right?

Lynn I said – wonderful.
Laurence Not *too* creased?

Lynn Perfect.

Look.

She indicates their image in the mirror.
That's us.
Laurence I know.

Lynn Are we . . . all right?
Laurence Are we all right?

Miles   Are we convincing?

Melanie   They *are* a bit creased.

Miles   Because I sometimes feel . . .

Pause.

Never mind.

Melanie   Come on.

She moves him towards the door.

Miles   Wait, wait.

He drags her back to the mirror.

I'll tell you something surprising . . .

That's not us . . .

Because that's not a mirror . . .

So that's not our room . . .

It's just like this one . . .

Why, what's wrong?

Lynn   I just sometimes wish . . .

Pause.

I don't know . . .

Laurence   I'm starving.

He moves her towards the door.

Lynn   Come back.

She drags him back to the mirror.

Just suppose . . .

. . . that wasn't us.

That's a window . . .

We're looking into the next room . . .

All the same things . . .

Bed, look . . .

Trouser-press.

The irresponsibility about personal possessions . . .

The cocktails in the Groll . . .

And then suddenly . . .

There in the middle of it all . . .

These two.

Two complete strangers.

Who are they?

Never seen them before in our lives.

Look at them . . .

Funny-looking pair.

Laurence Don't look funny to me.

Melanie We did stop the papers?

Miles No, but what do we think?

Lynn Are they nice? Are they nasty?

Sort of people we want to know?

Laurence You've got a funny way of looking at things, my pet.

Melanie You always want to

see things differently from other people.

He waves at his reflection.

Miles Hello!

Melanie Come on.

Miles No, but they're waving back.

She waves at her reflection.

Lynn Hello!

Laurence Come on.

Lynn Look, they want to be friends.

Melanie Dinner.

Laurence Eat.

Lynn Sorry, we've got to go.

Miles We don't want to know you after all.

They move towards the door.

They move towards the door. She stops.

Laurence Now what?

Lynn Just thinking.

Laurence Just thinking what?

Lynn What's going to be happening when we're not here?

Laurence What?

He stops.

Miles You know what's going to be going on in here while we're out?

Melanie No?

Miles No, nor do I.

Melanie What are you talking about?

Lynn No one pressing their trousers.

Miles No one reading the notices.

She opens the door.

He opens the door.

Laurence Right, off we go.

Melanie I'm going.

Lynn No one looking at themselves in the mirror.

Miles No one looking at anything.

Nothing will be happening.

So what'll be happening?

Nothing at all.

Melanie (*to* **Laurence**) Good evening.

Laurence (*to* **Melanie**) Oh – hello.

(*To* **Miles**.) Come on. I don't want to stand there in the corridor all evening.

(*To* **Lynn**.) Buck up. There's people out here waiting to come by.

Miles Not even anything existing . . .

Lynn Nothing . . .

He shudders, switches off the lights, and goes out. The door closes. Darkness. Then it immediately re-opens, and the lights come up again as **Miles** *enters. He looks round the room. Enter* **Melanie**.

Melanie   What in heaven's name is it now?

Miles   Just checking.

Melanie   Checking what?

Miles   That it's all still here.

Melanie (*coldly*)   Oh, and is it?

Miles   It saw me coming.

He ushers her out, and switches off the light. Darkness. Music. Then the bedside lights come up as **Melanie** *opens the door.*

Melanie (*politely*) Good night!

Miles (*politely*)   Good night!

She comes in, switching on the main lights. He follows, closing the door.

Miles   Kevin and Sharon!

The original Kevin and Sharon!
He flings himself down on the bed.

She shudders, switches off the lights, and goes out. The door closes. Darkness.

Music. Then the bedside lights come up as **Laurence** *opens the door.*

Laurence (*genially*)   Night night, then!

Lynn (*genially*)   Sleep tight!

He comes in, switching on the main lights. She follows, closing the door.

Laurence   What a Nigel!

Nigel and Nigella!

Nigel and Nigella Prat!

Why is it that one's fellow-countrymen abroad are so embarrassing?

Kind of people who make you feel ashamed to be British.

Melanie   Do you want the bathroom?

Miles   'After you, Sharon.' 'Oh, ta ever so, Kevvy.'

She goes into the bathroom.

Lynn   At least they were saying something to each other. At least they weren't sitting there in total silence.

She goes into the bathroom. He undresses.

Laurence   No – he never stopped! Voice you can hear halfway across the restaurant. Snigger, snigger, snigger, about everything. Something funny about the music, something funny about the tablecloths. Soup doesn't come up to his high standards. They've done something comic with the fish. I thought we were never going to hear the last of the sweet trolley. And he thinks *he's* not comic? He's the comicest thing of the lot! All this sniffing the wine, all this swilling it round. You hear what he said? 'Full and fruity, with just a hint of moles' armpits.'

Lavatory flush. She comes out of the bathroom to fetch something.

Miles   I think they're talking about us. Kevin and Sharon. I can hear a low indignant burbling coming through the wall.

Melanie   His name's Laurence.

Miles   Laurence?

Melanie   She called him Laurence.

Miles   Laurence . . .

Melanie   Nothing funny about being called Laurence, is there?

She goes back into the bathroom.

Miles   Nothing at all. Wonderful name. Saint Laurence. Laurence of Arabia . . . . What's she called?

Melanie (*off*)   Lynn.

Miles   Lynn? Did you say Lynn? Laurence and *Lynn*?

Lavatory flush. She comes out of the bathroom

Lynn   What?

Laurence   What?

Lynn   I thought you said something.

Laurence   I did. I said, 'Full and fruity, with just a hint of old jockstraps.'

She appears from the bathroom.

Melanie I should keep your voice down.

Miles They can't hear.

Melanie I can hear *them*.

Miles What, in the bathroom? You mean peeing?

She goes back into the bathroom.

Or worse? All right, I don't want to embarrass them. I'll call them Kevin and Sharon. I don't know how you heard they were called Laurence and Lynn. They scarcely said a word all the way through dinner. Just sat there avoiding each other's eye.

She comes out of the bathroom and undresses.

Melanie Yes, because they knew you were looking at them.

Miles I wasn't looking at them.

Melanie You obviously were.

Miles I was listening to them.

Melanie You can't have been listening to them, because you were talking all the time.

Miles *You* were listening to them.

She goes back into the bathroom.

Melanie *I* wasn't listening to them.

Miles You must have been listening to them – you heard them say something to each other. 'Oh, Laurence!' 'Oh, Lynn!' A conversation which passed me by completely, even though I was straining my ears.

Melanie She said, 'Laurence, do you want coffee?'

Miles Oh, how romantic. I'm sorry I missed that. And he replied, 'Oh, no, Lynn, no coffee for me, my precious. All I want is you.'

Melanie Aren't you going to get undressed?

Miles Ooh, Sharon, you saucy piece! I'll clean my teeth ever so quick!

He goes into the bathroom.

She comes out of the bathroom.

Laurence 'Full and fruity, with just a hint of ponces' arseholes.'

Lynn He was making a joke.

Laurence Oh, really?

Lynn It's what it said in the wine-list.

Laurence 'Just a hint of raspberries.' I know, he read it out. Twice.

Lynn Have you cleaned your teeth?

Laurence   He read out most of the wine-list.

He goes into the bathroom.

Lynn   I thought it was quite funny.

Laurence (*off*)   I know. I saw you laugh.

Lynn   I didn't laugh.

Laurence (*off*)   *He* saw you laugh.

Lynn   I didn't laugh!

Laurence (*off*)   He was doing it for your benefit!

Lavatory flush.
She gets into bed.

Melanie   I thought they were a rather sweet couple. I don't know why you have to keep putting everyone down.

Lynn   I don't know why you're so cross if anything makes me laugh. I thought they seemed a nice couple.

At least he didn't keep talking all the time, he didn't keep making jokes. They could just sit there in peace.

At least he was saying something. At least he was making a few jokes. They could sit there and have a good time together.

I don't know why you can't just quietly enjoy things for a moment.

She gets into bed.

I wish *you'd* got a bit more sense of humour.

Laurence *comes out of the bathroom, cleaning his teeth.*

Laurence   You telling me I haven't got a sense of humour?

Lynn   Well, you're not a *great* one for jokes, are you?

Laurence   Jokes? You want jokes? There's this feller goes into a bar . . .

Lynn   Stop cleaning your teeth for a moment, then.

Laurence   There's this feller goes into a bar. Right?

Lynn   Right.

Laurence   No, there's this feller sitting in a bar, and this feller comes in, this other feller.

Lynn   Why don't you have a little practice on your own first?

Laurence   Feller walks up the wall, right? Feller who's come in. Feller watches him. Feller in the bar. Feller walks across the ceiling. OK? Walks down the other wall and out of the bar. Feller in the bar says: 'That's funny, he didn't say Good evening.'

Lynn   You've got toothpaste on your chin.

Laurence   The *barman* says: 'That's funny, he didn't say Good evening.'

Lynn   Have you flushed?

He goes back into the bathroom. Lavatory flush.

Miles *comes out of the bathroom.*

Miles   The imagination boggles at what old Kevin's up in that bathroom.

Melanie   What are you talking about?

Miles   Cleans his teeth, then flushes the loo. I know people get a little confused about the functions of the *bidet*, but cleaning your teeth in the lavatory . . . .

He undresses.

Melanie   Will you do something?

Miles   What do you want?

Melanie   We're on holiday.

Miles   Yes?

Melanie   Special treat. For me.

Miles   OK.

Melanie   Say something serious.

Miles   All right.

Melanie   Just one thing.

Miles   One thing . . .
Anything?

Melanie   Anything.

Miles   Bright's Disease.

Melanie   Thank you.

He gets into bed.

Miles   I expect old Kevin's
being serious.

Laurence *comes out of the
bathroom.*

Laurence   *Dog* walks into a
bar . . .

Lynn   Light.

Laurence   Says to the
barman . . .

Lynn   Light. In the bathroom.
It's on.

He turns out the bathroom light.

Laurence   You'd better move
in with Nigel, then. I expect
he's telling jokes.

He puts his ear to the wall.

Miles   Gone very quiet in
there.

He puts his ear to the wall.

Melanie   What are you
doing?

Lynn   What are you doing?

Laurence   (*voice down*)   No one

saying anything at all in there, I'll tell you that.

Miles (*voice down*)   Bit of serious whispering going on.

Bit of whispering, that's all.

Lynn   I don't think that's very nice.

Melanie   That's a horrible thing to do.

Miles   Sh!

Laurence   Sh!

He's saying something . . .

What's he saying?

'Oh, Sharon, I love you!'

He takes his head away from the wall and gazes at it in mock surprise.

He takes his head away from the wall and gazes at it in surprise.

He reapplies his ear to the wall.

Lynn   What?

'Oh, Kevin, I love you, too!'

He reapplies his ear to the wall.

He starts away from the wall again in mock surprise.

He starts away from the wall again. He laughs.

Lynn   What? What's going on?

Laurence   No sense of humour? What about this, then? Old Nigel and Nigella in there . . .

He puts his ear back to the wall, and starts away again in genuine surprise.

He laughs.

Miles   Good God.

Melanie   Why? What's happening?

Miles (*disconcerted*)   Laughing his head off.

Lynn   What? What?

Laurence   Know what they're called? Kevin and Sharon!

He turns out the light. Darkness.

He turns out the light. Darkness. Pause. Lights on again. He is sitting up in bed, looking round the room.

Melanie   Now what?

Miles   Just checking.

He turns the lights out again. Darkness.

Laurence   Kevin and Sharon!

Lynn   Very funny.

Laurence   All right – tell you something else, then.

Lynn   No more jokes tonight.

Laurence   No, something serious.

Lynn   Bit of sleep first.

Pause.

Laurence   I love you.

Pause.

I said I love you.

Lynn   Um.

Pause.

Miles   You know I love you?

Melanie (*coolly*)   Do you?

Miles   You know I do. It's the Kevin and Sharon story all over again.

Melanie   Oh.

Miles   No, I'm saying something serious. I'm trying to say something serious. I *am* saying something serious.

Melanie   Oh, good.

Miles   So how about you?

Melanie   What?

Miles   Do you love me?

Melanie   Yes.

Miles   Yes?

Melanie   I've said – yes!

Lights on.

Melanie   Now what?

Miles   Just checking.

Melanie   Do stop this!

Miles   No, the expression on your face when you say that.

She turns out the light.

Lynn   Laurence? You're not asleep, are you?

Laurence   Um?

Lynn   Laurence . . .

Laurence   What's the matter?

Lynn   I love you, too.

Pause. Lights on. She is sitting up in bed.

Laurence   What? I said! I said before!

Lynn   Mosquito.

Laurence   Mosquito?

Lynn   I heard it.

Laurence   I can't hear anything.

Lynn   I heard it!

Laurence   Gone.

Lynn   It'll be back.

Laurence   Get some sleep.

Lynn   Soon as we put the lights out.

She puts the lights out.

Laurence   Not a sound.

Lynn   I'm listening.

Laurence   Go to sleep.

Lynn   I'm waiting.

Lights on. He is sitting up in bed looking at her.

Miles   'Yes?' Just – 'yes'?

Melanie   What are you talking about?

Miles   I say, 'Do you love me?' And you just say 'yes', and turn out the lights?

Pause. Then she turns over and embraces him.

Melanie Come on, then.

Miles I didn't mean that.

Melanie Yes, you did. Come on. Quietly, though.

Miles Quietly, right.

Melanie Don't wake the whole hotel.

Miles Don't want to make Kevin and Sharon jealous.

Lights on. She is sitting up in bed, slapping at herself.

Lynn Get off! Get off!

Laurence What, back?

Lynn I felt it go in! Look, blood! There's blood on the sheet!

Oh dear. Bit of competition.

Melanie Never mind them. Go on if you're going to.

There! There!

She jumps up on the bed, pointing at the ceiling, and pulls the duvet round her. He gets to his feet.

Laurence Where?

Lynn There!

He fetches a towel, and attempts to track the mosquito as it moves about the room.

Up here . . . ! Down there . . . ! No . . . Yes!

Laurence   Oh, right . . . You little devil!

He enters into the spirit of the chase.

Lynn   Give me another one . . .

He hands her another towel.

Laurence   Here!

Slaps the towel at it.

Lynn   There!

Slaps.

Laurence   Where?

They rain a fusillade of slaps.

Miles   What – flagellation?

Melanie   Don't listen.

Miles   Don't listen?

Lynn   Nearly!

Laurence   Wor!

Lynn   Careful!

Laurence   Wallop! Wallop!

Lynn   Wait, wait . . . Now!

Laurence   Ah!

Lynn   Yes! No . . .

They pause, panting, searching.

Miles   We should have guessed. They look so abnormally normal . . .

Melanie · They've finished.

Miles   Have they?

Melanie   Go on.

Miles   I'm listening.

Melanie   Silence.

Miles   Right . . .

They both cry out, pointing at the ceiling over the bed. They jump wildly about all over the bed, grunting and shouting, trying to reach the mosquito as it moves around the ceiling.

Laurence   Gotcher!

Lynn   Gotcher!

Laurence   Very satisfactory.

Lynn   That's my blood on the ceiling.

They settle down in bed.

Laurence   Know what?

Lynn   What?

Laurence   I enjoyed that.

Miles *reaches for the light switch.*

Melanie   No?

Miles   No.

He turns out the light.
Music, as before. The crash of a tablelamp falling over.

He turns out the light.
Music, as before.

Melanie (*sleepily*)   What's happening?

Miles   Nothing. Go back to sleep.

Melanie   Turn on the light.

Miles   That *was* the light.

More noises in the darkness.

Melanie   What time is it?

Miles   Quarter past three.

Melanie   What are you doing?

Miles   Trying not to disturb you.

Pause. Then a crash, a cry of pain, and the noise of a gunfight, very loud. Dramatic music. Shouts in Rewindese.

Melanie   Oh, my God!

He turns out the light.

He turns on the light.

Laurence   There's a riot going on!

He is on his hands and knees in his suitcase.

Melanie   What in the name of heaven . . . ?

Miles   Suitcase!

Not the car? They're not attacking the car?

He jumps out of bed and hurries to the window to look.

Melanie   You've turned the TV on!

Miles   I fell on the remote!

Melanie   Turn it off!

Miles   I'm trying to! I can't find it!

Melanie You'll wake the whole hotel!

Lynn It's next door! They've gone mad!

She hammers on the wall.

It's next door! You've woken them up!

He hunts through spilled clothes.

Miles I can't find the remote!

You'll have to go and talk to them!

He storms out of the door, followed by her.

Melanie What's this?

She retrieves the remote.

Miles That's it!

Thundering on the door. He goes to open it.

Melanie Which button?

Miles The top one!

The sound redoubles in intensity, as **Miles** *opens the door.* **Laurence** *stands on the threshold, with* **Lynn** *behind him.*

Laurence Look, I'm sorry, but it's three o'clock in the morning . . . !

Miles I know, I know! (*To* **Melanie**.) The top one, the top one!

*The sound redoubles in intensity
again.* **Miles** *comes hurrying back
to help, followed by* **Laurence** *and*
Lynn.

The bottom one!

*The sound switches to low-grade
Rewindese porn, hugely loud.*

Oh my God . . . ! The blue one!
The red one!

Lynn (*screams*)   The one that
says 'off'!

Silence. Pause.

Miles   I'm so sorry.

Laurence   I thought we'd got
a riot going on!

Miles   I am most abjectly
apologetic.

Lynn   He thought it was the
car! He thought they'd got the
cars!

Miles   I fell on the remote. I
do most humbly and contritely
apologise.

Melanie   But . . . what were
you *doing*?

Miles   I was trying not to
disturb you.

Melanie   I know. But . . .

Miles   Looking for the
bathroom.

*He feels along the downstage left
wall to demonstrate.*

Couldn't find the door.

Melanie The bathroom's over here!

She points to it, upstage. **Miles** *looks at it, then back at the downstage left wall.*

Miles It was here last night.

Laurence Well, if you're OK . . .

Laurence *and* **Lynn** *execute a withdrawal.*

Melanie I'm terribly sorry.

Miles Extremely sorry.

Lynn No, sorry to come bursting in.

Melanie Very sorry.

Laurence No, only it's three o'clock in the morning . . .

Miles Dreadfully sorry.

He closes the door. Pause.

Melanie I'll put it up here. The remote. You won't fall on it up here?

She gets back into bed.

Laurence *and* **Lynn** *enter.*

Lynn Moved the bathroom? And then he turns the telly on? At three o'clock in the morning? *What* are they called?

Laurence (*shortly*) Kevin and Sharon.

Lynn Very funny pair. You're right.

I *told* you not to leave the suitcase there.

Miles Last night the suitcase was *here*. The bathroom was *there* . . .

Melanie Aren't you going, then? After all that?

Miles *This* was the suitcase – *that* was the bathroom.

She lies down and turns away from him.

Miles Turn the light out, then.

He goes into the bathroom.

Melanie What, and start all over again?

Miles (*off*) I'm there now. Go back to sleep!

Melanie It's not anything to laugh about, you know. Waking everyone up. Spoiling their holiday. Making a complete fool of yourself.

They get back into bed.

I said you're right.

Laurence I heard you.

Lynn I thought you'd be laughing.

Laurence Did you?

He turns off the light.

She turns on the light.

Lynn   Go on, then.

Laurence   What?

Lynn   What have I done wrong?

Laurence   What do you mean?

Lynn   I've done something wrong. I've said the wrong thing.

Laurence   Let's get some sleep.

He turns the light out. She turns the light on.

Lynn   What was it?

Laurence   Forget it.

He turns the light out. She turns the light on.

Lynn   What, the car? Because I said about the car?

Laurence   *Someone's* got to think about the car!

Lynn Fine, good, think about the car, nobody's stopping you!

Laurence You don't have to go shouting it out to everyone in the world!

He turns the light out.

He comes out of the bathroom.

Miles   I said turn out the light. If you want to go to sleep.

She sits up in bed.

Melanie I feel very embarrassed.

Miles *You* feel embarrassed?

Melanie You're always doing this kind of thing.

Miles I have never before mistaken the position of a hotel bathroom.

Melanie You've fallen over your suitcase.

Miles But never on to the remote control of a television set.

Melanie You're always . . . shouting . . . and making jokes . . . and crashing about . . . !

Miles Sh!

Melanie Are *you* shushing *me*?

He gestures at her to keep her voice down.

You think they've got back to sleep after all that? I'll tell you what they're doing. They're talking about us.

She turns the light on.

Lynn What, you think they're lying there talking about you?

Laurence I don't care what they're doing.

Miles I might have expected a bit of sympathy, a bit of loyalty. I could have broken my leg.

I just don't like you shooting your mouth off about me to all and sundry.

I do in fact have a rather painful bruise on my elbow. Never mind, though. Sleep well.

He lies down and turns his back.

Melanie   I wonder if *he* treats *her* like this?

She turns out the light. Darkness. A phrase of music. Then grey light – pink light – dawn.

He lies down and turns his back.

Lynn   I wonder if *he* treats *her* like this?

She turns out the light. Darkness. A phrase of music. Then grey light – pink light – dawn.

She sits up.

Lynn (*alarmed*)   What time is it?

She finds her watch.

Miles *sits up.*

Miles (*alarmed*)   Where are we?

Lynn (*looking at her watch*)   Are we ahead or are we behind?

Melanie (*wakes*)   What? What is it?

Miles   I can't remember which country we're in!

Melanie   Don't start.

Miles   Oh yes. It's the Place with the Trouser-press.

He gets up, and orients himself.

Trouser-press ... suitcase ...
car-park ...

He looks round carefully.

He gets up and heads straight for the window.

Lynn   What, the car?

Laurence   What?

Lynn   You're going to look at the car?

Laurence   I'm on my way to the bathroom.

He diverts sharply to the bathroom.

All right?

Miles   Bathroom! All right?

Melanie   I said, Don't start.

He goes into the bathroom. She gets up.

She gets up.

Lynn (*concessive*)   Don't worry. *I'll* have a look.

What sort of day is it?

She goes out on to the balcony.

She goes out on to the balcony.

Melanie   Oh. Sorry!

Lynn   Sorry!

Melanie *goes back inside again.* **Lynn** *gazes down at the car-park.* **Melanie** *goes out on to the balcony again.*

Melanie   Sorry about all the performance in the night.

Lynn   Oh, no. We just didn't know what was happening. He thought it was the revolution breaking out.

Melanie   I was so embarrassed.

Lynn   No, mine's just as bad. Night before last, middle of the night, he gets up, and yes, he finds the bathroom, no problem, but then what happens? – I don't know – he won't turn the light on – he starts crashing about – I say 'For heaven's sake turn the light on!' – he *won't* turn the light on – next thing I know everything's going smash, crash . . . I go running in – the floor's covered in broken glass – and he starts shouting at *me* – somehow it's all *my* fault!

She peers.

Melanie   What – your car?

Lynn   See if it's all right. I got into hot water over that, too. Shouldn't have said he was worried about it. He was *furious!*

Melanie   *He* was furious! I don't know what *he'd* got to be furious about. I *told* him not to leave his suitcase there!

Lynn   Wouldn't speak, mine!

Melanie   I quite like it when they won't speak.

Lynn *peers.* **Melanie** *looks as well.*

Melanie   Which one is it?

Lynn   I can't remember.

Melanie   What colour is it?

Lynn   I've forgotten. What colour's yours?

Melanie   Search me.

Lynn   I don't know what we're doing here, tell you the truth.

Melanie   *I* don't know what we're doing here!

Lynn   I don't know where we're going!

Melanie   *I* don't know where we're going!

Lynn   *He* dreamed all this up!

Melanie   Supposed to be a break for me.

Lynn   I'd rather put my feet up with a good book.

Melanie   I just want to get on with my work.

Lynn   I suppose *they* like it.

Melanie   Do they?

Lynn   Don't they?

Melanie   Not much evidence of it.

Lynn   He gets in such a state about it.

Melanie   He never wants to *meet* anyone.

Lynn   Never wants to *meet* anyone!

They realise that **Laurence** *and* **Miles** *have come out of the bathroom, and are watching them.*

Melanie   Oh, here he is.

Lynn   He's giving me a very funny look.

Melanie   He'll think we're talking about him.

Lynn   They always think you're talking about them!

Melanie   See you in breakfast, perhaps.

Lynn *and* **Melanie** *go back inside.*

Miles   So how's Sharon this morning?

Melanie   Fine.

Miles   Telling you all about Kevin?

Melanie   Have you finished in the bathroom?

Laurence   So how's the car?

Lynn   The car?

Laurence   I thought you were looking at the car?

Lynn   The car's fine.

Miles   Or were you telling her all about me?

Melanie   What colour's our car?

Miles   They haven't broken into it?

Melanie   I said what colour is it?

Miles   They haven't *taken* it?

He goes out on to the balcony.

He goes out on to the balcony.

Lynn   Don't you believe me?

Laurence   See what sort of day it is . . .

Laurence   Oh – hello!

Miles   Sorry – just checking the car's still there.

Laurence   OK?

Miles   Seems to be. Yours all right?

Laurence   Hadn't thought. Let's have a look. Yes, still there. Still got four wheels.

Miles   Sorry about . . . you know . . . in the night.

Laurence   No, I sympathise. Diabolical, the way they move the bathrooms around in these places. You'd think they'd standardise. You'd think

Brussels would do something.

Miles   Have the same layout everywhere.

Laurence   By law.

Miles   TV here, bathroom there.

Laurence   You find the bathroom – you *still* don't know where you are. One night you've got the basin here, you've got the loo there. Next night – the basin's here, the loo's there.

Miles   You get up in the middle of the night . . .

Laurence   Night before last. Don't want to disturb *her* . . .

Miles   So you don't turn the light on . . .

Laurence   Don't turn the light on. And there I am in the bathroom, bending down . . .

Miles   Feeling for the loo . . .

Laurence   Feeling for the loo . . .

Miles   Which in fact is behind you . . .

Laurence   Which in fact is behind me . . .

Miles   So your head . . .

Laurence   Unknown to me . . .

Miles   Is in the basin.

Laurence   Suddenly . . .

Miles   Thump!

Laurence   Hot tap – *here*, over my right eye.

Miles   Right eye?

Laurence   Right eye. Jump up . . .

Miles   Don't tread on the remote . . .

Laurence   Don't tread on the remote, no,

because the remote's not in the bathroom. Worse.
Hit the back of my head against the shelf over
the basin.

Miles   Crack!

Laurence   Glass shelf.

Miles   Of course.

Laurence   Not fixed.

Miles   Certainly not.

Laurence   Loose on its brackets.

Miles   Naturally.

Laurence   Plus various glass tumblers, pots of
face cream et cetera, make-up mirror et cetera et
cetera.

Miles   Glass everywhere.

Laurence   All over the floor.

Miles   Bare feet.

Laurence   In the dark.

Miles   Your wife comes running.

Laurence   'What are you playing at?'

Miles   'You'll wake the whole hotel!'

Laurence   'Don't come in! Don't move! Just
turn the light on!'

Miles   'Where's the light?'

Laurence   'Can't find the light!'

Miles   Total panic.

Laurence   They should standardise the light
switches.

Miles   Put your hand out, no matter where you
are.

Laurence   Spain, France, Luxembourg.

Miles   On comes the light.

Laurence   I mean, it wasn't my idea in the first place.

Miles   Going on holiday?

Laurence   I'd just as soon do the garden, quite frankly.

Miles   I shouldn't mind working, to tell you the truth. I quite like working.

Laurence   But you put yourself out.

Miles   Whatever you do you know it's not going to be right.

Laurence   Ah well.

Miles   There you go.

Laurence   What would we do without them?

Miles   Holidays?

Laurence   No ...

He nods in the direction of the room. **Lynn** *and* **Melanie** *are packing, and watching* **Laurence** *and* **Miles** *curiously.*

Miles   Oh. Yes. Right. What indeed?

Laurence   Bless their hearts.

Miles   Anyway, you got back to sleep in the end?

Laurence   Out like a light. You and Sharon?

Miles   Me and ... ?

Laurence   Sharon? Got a bit of sleep?

Miles   Oh – us – yes. Fine, fine.

Laurence   Well, better go and shave.

Miles   On into the great unknown.

Laurence   Wonder where the bathroom'll be tonight?

Miles   Touch of mystery to our lives.

Laurence   See you in breakfast?

Miles   Yes, you must meet Sharon.

Laurence   Been nice talking to you, Kevin.

Miles *and* **Laurence** *go back into their rooms.*

Melanie (*coolly*)   I'm glad you've found someone to talk to at last.

Miles   Me and Kevin? We're like that together.

Lynn (*coolly*)   Well, you seem to have found a soul-mate.

Laurence   What, old Kevin? He's all right.

We're having breakfast with them.

Thought we might all meet up over breakfast.

Lynn   Oh, well, this is a change.

She goes into the bathroom.

'We've all done it, Kevin. We've all been there. We've all had troubles with the bathroom. Women, Kevin? They're all alike.'

Melanie (*shocked*)   You didn't call him Kevin?

Miles I didn't call him Kevin. *He* called *me* Kevin.

Melanie *He* called *you* Kevin?

Miles 'You and Sharon get back to sleep all right, Kevin?' You're Sharon.

Melanie He called me Sharon?

Miles He wants to meet you properly over breakfast. Two Kevins – two Sharons – we're going to get on like a house on fire.

She gazes at him in horror.

She comes out of the bathroom, holding toilet stuff to pack.

Lynn Well, just as long as you don't go calling him Kevin.

Laurence What do you want me to call him? Nigel?

Lynn You didn't . . . ?

Laurence Didn't what?

Lynn Call him Kevin just now? You didn't call him Kevin out there?

Laurence Kevin, yes. Why not? Kevin. What's wrong?

She gazes at him in horror.

Melanie He heard you! Everything you said about them! He heard you!

Lynn He *told* you he's called Kevin?

Laurence I *know* he's called Kevin!

Lynn   Because you were listening through the wall, you turnip!

Come on – finish packing! Let's get out of here!

Miles   Breakfast . . .

Melanie   I couldn't look them in the eye!

Miles   Come on – be reasonable.

Melanie   I *am* being reasonable!

Miles   We'll make a joke of it.

Melanie   *They've* made the joke of it already. Somebody else making the jokes for once. Close your case up.

She hurls together the last of the packing.

She hurls together the last of the packing.

We'll get breakfast on the road somewhere.

Laurence   We've paid for breakfast here.

Lynn   What, and sit there with Kevin and Sharon, and them knowing we've had our ear to the wall?

Quick, before we meet them in the corridor!

Come on, or we'll be meeting them in the corridor!

That the lot?

Have we got everything?

Come on.

They open the door, and struggle out with their luggage.

They open the door, and struggle out with their luggage.

Buck up, buck up!

Oh, hello!

Hello!

Miles   Thought we'd give breakfast a miss, after all.

Laurence   Us, too.

Hit the road.

Beat the traffic.

Melanie   Hold on. Just check we've got everything . . .

Lynn   See if we've left anything behind . . .

She pushes him back into the room, and closes the door.

She pushes him back into the room, and closes the door.

Miles   What?

Laurence   What?

Lynn   Let them get out of the way first.

Melanie   Give them a head start.

Miles   I don't know why *they're* going.

Laurence   I don't know why *they're* going.

Melanie   (*grimly*)   Don't you?

Lynn   (*grimly*)   Don't you?

They wait.

They wait. She listens at the door.

Laurence   (*looks round the room*)   Bit of our life.

Miles (*looks round the room*) And so another chapter in the story closes behind us.

No sign we were ever here.

Melanie The lampshade wasn't that shape when we arrived . . .

They wait.

Miles They must have gone by now.

Actually, if they've gone . . .

We could have breakfast.

Melanie Don't be silly.

Miles Leave now, we'll bump into them in the car-park.

Pause. She puts her case down.

Lynn What?

Laurence I said it's a bit of our life. This room.

Lynn I know.

Laurence Haven't left anything?

Lynn Bit of my lifeblood up there on the ceiling . . .

They wait.

Laurence Listen . . . Silence.

If they've gone . . .

We could have breakfast.

Lynn I just want to get out of here.

Laurence They'll still be paying their bill.

Pause. She puts her case down.

Melanie Quickly, then . . .

Miles Breakfast?

Lynn Breakfast.

She flings the door open and goes out,
then bundles him back inside again.

She flings the door open and goes out,
then bundles him back inside again.

I knew it, I knew it!

Melanie Why do I ever
listen to anything you say?

She picks up the bags.

She picks up the bags.

Come on!

Laurence But . . .

Miles If they're still . . .

Lynn I don't care! Just get
out of here!

Melanie Out, out, out, out!

They go straight out with all the
luggage.

They go straight out with all the
luggage.

Melanie (*merrily*) Change of
plan!

Lynn (*merrily*) Change of plan!

Miles You too?

Laurence You too?

Melanie Never get away
from each other again!

Lynn Never get away from
each other again!

Miles *and* **Melanie**
(*together*) Doomed to be
doubles!

Laurence *and* **Lynn**
(*together*) Doomed to be
doubles!

They cast one last haggard look back
into the room, then go out, laughing,
and close the door. Darkness.

They cast one last haggard look back
into the room, then go out, laughing,
and close the door. Darkness.

Act Two

Leavings

Table and chairs. **John, Jocasta, Nicholas** *and* **Nancy.**

Nancy*'s arm is in a sling.* **John** *is asleep.*

Pause.

Nicholas Well . . .

Nancy Well . . .

Pause.

Jocasta Shall I make some more coffee?

Nicholas No, we really ought to be . . .

Nancy (*looks at her watch*) Oh, my God, yes – look at the time!

Nicholas (*looks at his watch*) How did it get to be so late?

Pause.

Nancy We were going to be going half an hour ago.

Nicholas Yes – how come we're still sitting here?

Pause.

Nancy Well, then . . .

Nicholas (*looks at* **John**) We must let these good people get some sleep.

Jocasta (*to* **John**) Darling . . .

Nicholas Don't wake him.

Nancy Busy day.

Nicholas Privilege of the host.

Nancy We'll just quietly slip away.

Pause.

Jocasta   You don't have to go dashing off.

Nicholas   Some of us have got to get up in the morning.

Pause.

Jocasta   Well, if you've really got to . . .

Nicholas   Come on, then.

Nancy   Lovely evening.

Nicholas *and* **Nancy** *push their chairs back.*

Jocasta (*nudges* **John**; *firmly*)   Darling . . . They're leaving . . .

John (*wakes up*)   Yes, we've got to be going. (*Looks at his watch.*) Oh my God, look at the time!

Jocasta   Darling!

John   How did it get to be so late? Some of us have got to get up in the morning! Come on, then.

He gets to his feet.

Lovely evening. We must let these good people get some sleep . . .

He stops, confused.

Jocasta   Honestly!

Nicholas   Well, if you've really got to . . .

John   No, no . . .

Nicholas   We mustn't stop you.

Jocasta   You live here. Remember?

John   No, no, no, no . . .

Jocasta   What do mean, no, no, no, no?

Nancy   Don't worry! We can take a hint!

Nicholas *and* **Nancy** *get to their feet.*

John   I mean, *you* sit down! Go on – sit down, sit down, sit down, sit down! Have another glass of wine!

He refills their glasses.

Jocasta They were just going!

John Nonsense! Sit down!

Nicholas It's taken us an hour to get on our feet.

John Sit down!

Nicholas You slept through the entire negotiations!

John I wasn't asleep!

Nicholas He wasn't asleep.

John I was thinking.

Nicholas Deep in thought.

John About what you were saying. Sit down!

Nicholas What *were* we saying?

Nancy We weren't saying anything.

Nicholas Long silences.

Nancy While we were waiting for *you* to speak.

Nicholas That's how we knew it was time to go.

John About machines.

Nicholas About machines?

John About burglar alarms and answering machines.

Nicholas Oh, that!

Nancy Then!

Jocasta That was when we got back from casualty!

Nancy Was that this evening?

Nicholas Good God, have you been asleep since then?

John What you were saying . . .

Nancy   Bye bye.

Kisses him.

Thank you so much. I'm sorry about the . . . (*Indicates her arm.*)

Jocasta   No – all our fault.

Nancy   Don't come out.

Exit **Nancy** *left, followed by* **Jocasta**.

John   What you were saying . . .

Nicholas   Listen, we'll continue this another time.

John   . . . was that there was something unnatural about our dependence on all these machines.

Nicholas   Very enjoyable evening. Though actually that isn't what I was saying.

John   Oh, I thought it was.

Nicholas   We can't start all this again now, but as a matter of fact *you* were saying it was unnatural.

John   *You* were saying it was unnatural, and I was saying, no, what would be unnatural, now that these machines have been invented, now that they're actually in existence, would be *not* to use them.

Nicholas   No, what I was saying, what I was trying to say, was that it was very *natural* to use them . . .

John   'Unnatural' was the word you actually employed.

Nicholas   No, what I actually said was that it was only *too* natural . . .

John   Only too natural – exactly.

Nicholas   Only too natural doesn't mean unnatural.

John   Of course it does. Only too natural means *unnaturally* natural.

Nicholas   Unnaturally natural? This is an interesting concept . . .

He sits down.

John   What's odd about something being unnaturally natural?

Nicholas   What's odd about something being unnaturally natural? Look ... Sit down, sit down.

John *sits.*

Nicholas   Supposing I said something was naturally unnatural.

*Enter **Nancy** left.*

John   You might well say that.

Nancy   Oh no!

John   Something might well be naturally unnatural.

Nancy   You haven't sat down again?

Nicholas   Give me an example of something naturally unnatural.

*Enter **Jocasta** left.*

John   This table is naturally unnatural.

Jocasta   They've sat down again!

John   This glass is naturally unnatural.

Nancy   I thought we were going?

John   This chair is naturally unnatural.

Nancy   Come on!

Nicholas   You mean it's unnatural by nature?

John   I mean it's unnatural by nature.

Nicholas   Like an answering machine or a burglar alarm?

Nancy *sits down in exasperation.*

Nicholas   Don't start sitting down again! (*To **John**.*) Like an answering machine or a burglar alarm? (*To **Nancy**.*) I thought we were going?

Nancy *gets up.*

Nicholas (*to* **John**)   I thought you were arguing that they were natural?

Nancy *forces Nicholas up and propels him towards the door.* **John** *follows.*

John   Yes! Naturally natural!

Nicholas   But now you're saying they're naturally unnatural!

John   No, I'm not – I'm saying they're not unnaturally natural! No – not unnaturally unnatural . . . No, hold on . . .

Nicholas   I don't know what we're talking about.

John   *I* don't know what we're talking about.

Exit **Nicholas** *and* **John** *left.* **Nancy** *turns back to* **Jocasta.**

Nancy   Sorry. First they won't say anything . . .

Jocasta   Then they won't stop.

Nancy   I know – I meant to ask you about Ariadne . . .

Exit **Nancy** *left.* **Jocasta** *stops.*

Jocasta   You haven't heard?

Enter **Nancy** *left.*

Nancy   Heard what?

Jocasta   About Ariadne!

Nancy   No?

Jocasta   She's left Reggie.

Nancy   Left Reggie? Ariadne has left Reggie?

Jocasta   According to Joanna.

Nancy   What – somebody else?

Jocasta   You'll never guess! Grantley Forward!

Nancy   Grantley Forward? Reggie . . . and Grantley Forward?

Jocasta   Ariadne and Grantley Forward!

Nancy   No!

Jocasta   Yes!

Nancy   But I thought Grantley ...

Jocasta   With Georgina, yes. But you know that Georgina ...

Nancy   And Luciano ...

Jocasta   For years!

Nancy   For years!

Jocasta   Well, apparently he came back unexpectedly one day ...

Enter **Nicholas** *left, and waits with ostentatious patience.*

Nancy   Luciano?

Jocasta   Grantley! And found the two of them manacled to the bed together!

Nancy   Luciano and Georgina?

Jocasta   No!

Nicholas   John's standing on the pavement out there. They'll arrest him for loitering.

Nancy   Georgina and *Reggie*?

Jocasta   Amanda and Laurence!

Nancy   Amanda and Laurence? Who are they?

Jocasta   No one knows!

Nicholas *takes* **Nancy** *by the arm.*

Nicholas   It's like getting the couple in the weather house outdoors at the same time.

He kisses **Jocasta**.

Nancy   Amanda and Laurence?

Nicholas   No, no! Good night. Thank you so much. Loved the bit in casualty.

Exit **Nicholas** *and* **Nancy** *left.*

Nancy (*off*) But I don't understand . . .

Jocasta (*calls*) I'll give you a ring in the morning. Night night! Love to Charlie and Georgie!

Jocasta *yawns. Enter* **Nicholas** *left. She stops yawning.*

Nicholas You know Charlie got ninety-eight per cent in maths?

Jocasta Yes, Nancy said!

Nicholas He was so cross about it, though! He said, 'Dad, I got one wrong.' And when he showed me the paper . . .

Jocasta It was the the teacher who'd got it wrong!

Nicholas Sorry, sorry.

Jocasta No, no – nice to hear it confirmed. Night night.

Exit **Nicholas** *left. Enter* **Nicholas** *left, guiltily.*

Nicholas And Theodora? I meant to ask earlier.

Jocasta She's doing very well.

Nicholas The remedial reading . . . ?

Jocasta Is really helping. We're terribly pleased.

Enter **John** *left.*

John Have you two separated?

Nicholas Sorry. I was just asking about Theodora.

John What, this remedial caper?

Nicholas I gather it's really doing the trick.

John Yes – she can read quite long words now.

Nicholas Marvellous!

John Like the 'Play' on the video.

Jocasta She can read *all* the video controls.

John Except 'Stop'. She can't read 'Stop'.

Nicholas Anyway . . .

Jocasta What she needs is you to believe in what she's doing.

John What she needs is everyone to stop fussing.

Enter **Nancy** *left.*

Nancy You can see the stars moving out there if you watch for long enough.

Jocasta Sorry. We're talking about Theodora.

Nancy Oh, right.

John I mean, it's ridiculous. Some people are *natural* slow readers.

Nicholas *Naturally* natural slow readers?

John *Naturally* natural slow readers – yes.

Nancy I'll sit down.

She sits.

Nicholas Don't sit down! We're going, we're going!

Jocasta (*to* **Nicholas**) No, but bear me out! It's *not* natural not to be reading at her age! It's highly unnatural!

John It's not natural to read at any age!

Jocasta Oh, for heaven's sake!

John Reading is a highly unnatural activity.

Nicholas A *naturally* unnatural activity?

John A *naturally* unnatural activity.

Jocasta Oh, don't start all that again!

John But it is!

Jocasta Come on!

Exit **Jocasta** *left.*

John In fact it's an *unnaturally* unnatural activity . . .

Exit **John** *left.*

Nicholas You're still sitting there!

Nancy I want to be absolutely certain you're outside that door before I get to my feet.

Nicholas You're the one who keeps coming back!

Nancy Come on.

Nicholas It would make more sense . . .

He sits.

. . . if I stayed sitting down until *you* were outside that door.

Enter **Jocasta** *left. She gazes at* **Nicholas** *and* **Nancy** *in astonishment.*

Jocasta What?

Nicholas We're waiting.

Jocasta Waiting? What for?

Nancy Each other.

Nicholas Together. All right?

Nancy All right – together.

They get to their feet, watching each other. **Jocasta** *watches them.*

Nicholas Go on.

Nancy Together, yes?

Nicholas We can't get through the door together.

Nancy After you, then.

Nicholas After you.

Nancy Go on.

Nicholas No, no.

Jocasta *I'll* go.

Exit **Jocasta** *left.*

Nancy (*to* **Jocasta**) We're going to end up like those two manacled to the bed.

Exit **Nancy**.

Nicholas   What, Laurence Troon and Amanda Wivenhoe?

Enter **Nancy** *left.*

Nancy   It was Laurence *Troon?* And Amanda *Wivenhoe?*

Nicholas   According to George Worrall.

Nancy   You said you didn't know!

Nicholas   I didn't say anything.

Nancy   But this is terrible!

She pushes the door to.

Nicholas   What? What's happening?

Nancy   Amanda Wivenhoe lives with Charlie's maths tutor!

Nicholas   Yes, but he can't really complain. He's also involved
with that Kung Fu woman in Huddersfield . . .

Nancy   But if Charlie's maths tutor finds out about Amanda and
Laurence Troon . . .

She sits down.

. . . and moves in with the Kung Fu woman . . .

Nicholas   In Huddersfield . . . ?

Nancy   Then who do we get to tutor Charlie?

Nicholas   Oh my God!

He sits down.

Nancy   He doesn't know about Laurence Troon so far?

Nicholas   I've no idea.

Nancy   Who told you?

Nicholas   George Worrall.

Enter **Jocasta** *and* **John** *left.*

Nancy   Who presumably got it from Patsy.

Nicholas   Who will have told Clarissa.

Nancy   Who knows the Pillingtons.

Nicholas   Who may meet Charlie's maths tutor at the Muldews . . .

Nancy   We must make absolutely sure it doesn't go any further.

Nicholas   I won't tell a soul.

Nancy   Not a soul!

Nicholas   Not a soul!

John   Sorry. We just happened to be outside. Saw the front door was open – thought we'd drop in . . .

Nancy   Yes, sit down, sit down!

Nicholas   You're not going to believe this . . .

Nancy (*to* **Nicholas**)   Not a *soul!*

Nicholas   Not a *soul!*

Nancy   It was Laurence Troon and Amanda Wivenhoe!

Jocasta   You mean . . . ?

Nancy   Yes!

Jocasta   No!

She sits. **John** *watches them.*

Nicholas   And Amanda Wivenhoe lives with Charlie's maths tutor!

Nancy   Who's also involved with this woman in Huddersfield . . .

Nicholas   Who teaches Kung Fu!

Nancy   Who teaches Kung Fu!

Nicholas   So what's going to happen?

Nancy   He's going to leave Amanda . . .

Nicholas   And go zooming up to Huddersfield!

John Laurence Troon?

Nancy
Nicholas } Charlie's maths tutor!
Jocasta

John (*resignedly*) Oh, Charlie's maths tutor.

He sits.

Nancy Another glass of wine?

Nicholas Or something to eat?

Nancy I feel suddenly kind of hollow inside.

John How about breakfast?

Nicholas I'll do it!

Nancy I'll do it!

Nicholas Scrambled eggs?

Nancy A bit of bacon?

Jocasta Well . . .

John Actually . . .

Nicholas No, no!

Nancy You sit there . . .

Nicholas . . . and make yourselves at home . . . !

Curtain.

Look Away Now

Three aircraft seats.

Three passengers sitting in them: **Aptly**, **Bloss** *and* **Charr**.

Reassuring music. It suddenly stops.

Stewardess (*off, over PA*)   Now will you please ensure that your seat belt is securely fastened, ready for take-off.

Passengers **Aptly** *and* **Charr** *gaze absently and expressionlessly into space.* **Charr** *yawns. Passenger* **Bloss**, *between them, automatically checks the items mentioned.*

Stewardess   Your table should be folded away, with the seat-back upright and the arm-rest down. Your mind should be in the closed position to be adopted when routine safety announcements of this sort are made.

Aptly *glances at him, and he stops.*

Stewardess   If you are still conscious at this time, you may find the level tone of voice in which this announcement is being made helpful in securing complete inattention. In the pocket in front of you you will find a card showing aircraft safety procedures.

Bloss *automatically moves to look for the card.* **Aptly** *glances at him again, and he sits back and gazes into space.*

Stewardess   In the interest of your own peace of mind, please studiously ignore this. Any attempt to look at it may result in your appearing nervous or inexperienced to your fellow-passengers. We are mentioning it purely as a test to make sure that no one is listening.

The cabin attendants will now demonstrate the use of the aircraft's emergency oxygen masks and life jackets.

Aptly *and* **Charr** *immediately open their newspapers and become absorbed in them.*

Stewardess   They are not trained in mime or the use of

theatrical properties, and they find this performance profoundly embarrassing. It is important to them to know that no one is watching. Faces should be completely obscured by newspapers, or eyes securely shut.

Seeing **Aptly** *and* **Charr**, **Bloss** *hastily opens his own newspaper.*

Stewardess   If for any reason the cabin air-supply should fail, oxygen will be provided. Masks like this will appear automatically. We say 'like this', but what in fact these masks are like you have of course no idea.

Bloss *happens to glance over the top of his paper, and does a double-take. His mouth falls open.*

Stewardess   In the unlikely event of anyone looking up and finding out, please remain seated. Place the newspaper back in front of your face and try to breathe normally.

Bloss *lifts the newspaper in front of his face again.*

Stewardess   The action of pulling the mask to the face automatically opens the way to less inhibited behaviour. This may be required after a landing on water, when you will find that you have no idea where your life jacket is stowed.

Bloss *peers cautiously round the edge of his newspaper, amazed at the sight that meets his eyes.*

Stewardess   To prepare for immersion, check that your shirt is free from the waistband of the trousers or skirt, then pull it upwards over the head in one steady movement, like this. It is particularly important that no one watches any part of what follows.

Bloss *hurriedly vanishes again.*

Stewardess   Release the catch at the waistband, pull down the fastener provided, and let the lower garments fall to the floor. Please ensure that they do not obstruct the emergency exits.

Bloss *emerges from his newspaper again, vanishes in horror, then slowly re-emerges as his newspaper sinks, and gazes in covert fascination.*

Stewardess   There is a whistle attached to your lifejacket for attracting attention, which attendants are holding close to their lips, but being very careful not to blow in case attention should actually be attracted.

Bloss *looks at* **Aptly** *and* **Charr** *to see if they have seen what he has seen, but they are still deep in their newspapers. He gazes open-mouthed at the demonstration.*

Stewardess   Your whistle is of course still under your seat with the lifejacket, and you may wish to try alternative methods of persuading people to look at you. Your cabin attendants are now demonstrating the procedure for these. Ladies should undo the fastenings at the front of the upper undergarment as shown, and pass it backwards over the shoulders, like this.

Aptly *glances up from his newspaper and sees* **Bloss** *watching. He is amused by* **Bloss**'s *naivety.* **Charr** *glances up as well.* **Aptly** *nods discreetly in the direction of* **Bloss**. **Charr** *smiles as well.*

Stewardess   Now, peel any hosiery downwards, like this, followed by the lower undergarment, taking care to keep the pelvis rotating at the same time, as shown. Once off, the undergarments may if desired be passed around various parts of the body, like this, then tossed lightly into the faces of potential rescuers, who may be engrossed in reading matter at least as deeply as passengers are now. If you are still wearing the masks at this time, you may wish to loosen your inhibitions even further, as attendants are now demonstrating.

Bloss *suddenly realises he is being watched and hastily snatches up his newspaper. It disintegrates into its various component pages.* **Aptly** *and* **Charr** *reimmerse themselves in their newspapers.*

Stewardess   If necessary, the pressure can be increased by applying the mouth to this mouthpiece, but gentlemen, no pipes or cigars, please. For your own safety and comfort, kindly do not inflame other passengers until you are outside the aircraft. Thank you for your complete lack of attention.

A faint suspicion that they are missing something has now come to **Aptly** *and* **Charr**.

Stewardess   Now please allow cabin staff a few seconds to retrieve their clothes and retire to the galley areas to dress.

They discreetly lower their papers and look. There is nothing to be seen. They glance in puzzlement at **Bloss.**

Stewardess   Then open your eyes, fold newspapers away . . .

Bloss *collapses the remains of his newspaper as best he can.*

Stewardess   . . . settle back in your seats . . .

He settles back into his seat, glances at **Aptly** *and* **Charr**, *then gazes into space.*

Stewardess   . . . and enjoy the flight.

He smiles slightly to himself.

Curtain.

Heart to Heart

A table, with glasses, bottles, etc.

A confused roar of party conversation. **Charmian** *is standing while a* **Waitress** *refills her glass.* **Clifford** *approaches, with a glass, as the* **Waitress** *goes. He and* **Charmian** *begin to talk, in the most natural and friendly manner, but we can't hear a word they say.*

Clifford [I don't think we've met.]

Charmian [Yes, I remember.]

Clifford [My name's Clifford. What's yours?]

Charmian [Oh, fine. Well, I had one of these kind of fluey colds that are going round, but otherwise . . . fine!]

Clifford [Oh, that's rather an unusual name.]

Charmian [No, completely. Thank you. And are you well?]

Clifford [I *think* – I don't know – but I think because my parents were great admirers of Clifford Curzon.]

Charmian [Oh, how miserable, but at least it doesn't last long.]

He looks around. She looks around as well. The noise of the party gradually fades away. They continue to talk, their voices still raised against the noise, and you begin to hear what they are saying.

Clifford [Do you think anybody in this room can hear what anyone else is saying?]

Charmian [I wonder if anyone here can hear a word anyone else is saying.]

Clifford Or are they just going through the motions?

Charmian I sometimes think they're all just going through the motions!

Clifford I suppose there's one person who must be able to hear what everyone's saying.

Charmian   *Completely* insane!

Clifford   And that's God!

Charmian   *Very* odd, when you come to think about it.

Clifford   He just tunes out everybody else, and there's you and me, say, as clear as a bell!

Charmian   *Such* hell! Why do we do it?

Clifford   Everyone smiling and nodding away.

Charmian   Away? Yes, we have. To Egypt, which was rather a lark!

Clifford   Like a drain, I should think, when He realises they haven't the slightest idea what they're smiling and nodding *about.*

Charmian   Oh, a *brief* bout. You mean, of tummy?

Clifford   Hilarious.

Charmian   Well, *mildly* hilarious. And *you?* Have *you* managed to get away yet?

Clifford   Not a word, no.

Charmian   Oh, marvellous!

Clifford   Not a single word you've uttered.

Charmian   How wonderful!

Clifford   Have you heard anything I've said?

Charmian   No ... no ... I don't think we have. Not *there* exactly. But you'd recommend it, would you?

Clifford   I know you're asking me something.

Charmian   Of course. Quite. I understand that.

Clifford   Is it Do I live round here? or is it Did I see some ghastly wild life programme on television?

Charmian   Oh, we *love* the wild life ones! How about you?

Clifford   Just up the road.

Charmian   No, we missed the one about the toad. So do you live round here?

Clifford   No, I didn't.

Charmian   Where are you, then?

Clifford   Because I hate them.

Charmian   Oh, the Stopfords live there! Tim and Lise! Do you know them?

Clifford   Yes! *Loathe* them!

Charmian   *Do* you? Tim and Lise?

Clifford   Chimpanzees, yes – they're the ones I loathe most.

Charmian   *Tremendously* old friends!

Clifford   All those disgusting tricks they get up to with bananas.

Charmian   Mad as hatters! But don't you find them such a *treat*?

Clifford   Me? Yes! *Longing* to eat! Anything to get out of *this* hell!

Charmian   Thistle? Their little girl? Isn't she an absolute *winner*?

Clifford   Well, it's *time* for dinner.

Charmian   All *go*!

Clifford   Well, let's! Yes! You mean – together?

Charmian   Oh, *tremendously* together! Don't you think?

Clifford   Love to! You mean – *now*?

Charmian   An *absolute* wow!

Clifford   Right! Yes! Why not? If that's all right with *you*?

Charmian   Us? Two girls. Five and three. Terribly hard work, of course, but we do have an au pair.

Clifford   *Any*where, provided we can get out of this *noise*.

Charmian   No – *girls*. How about you? Do you have any?

Clifford   *Completely* ready. Let's go.

Charmian   No?

Clifford   Yes! Fine!

Charmian   *Nine?*

Clifford   Absolutely! Except ... this is ridiculous ...

Charmian   No, very brave of you.

Clifford   ... I didn't quite catch your name.

Charmian   *Quite* a game, I should think. I can't imagine how you cope!

Clifford   Cope?

Charmian   I couldn't *begin* to cope!

Clifford   Braginta Cope?

Charmian   No! Couldn't *possibly* cope!

Clifford   Sorry – *Cosima* Cope. Yes? Cosima Cope?

Charmian   Oh, I see. Because of the *Pope?*

Clifford   Cosima *Pope*, right. Got there. Cosima *Pope.*

Charmian   But you're allowed to use the *rhythm* method, aren't you?

Clifford   So do I! We'll find a place where we can dance!

He takes her by the arm to go.

Well, I don't think *we* gave God any cause for amusement, did we? I think He'd have been rather impressed!

Charmian   Yes, come on, *I'd* need a rest if *I* had nine.

They come face to face with Peter.

Peter (*to* **Clifford**)   Hello, I don't think we've met.

Clifford   Yes, I remember.

Peter   I'm Peter.

Clifford   You're David.

Peter   Peter Spatchworth.

Clifford   David, David . . . Don't tell me . . . Isn't it Hopper?

Peter   Sweltering. And you've met my wife?

Clifford   No.

Peter   No?

Clifford   She's away in Belgium, unfortunately.

Peter   Oh, well, let me introduce you.

Clifford   Of course. Cosima. Cosima Pope. But we've got to be popping.

Peter   Poppin? *You* are?

Clifford   Sadly.

Peter (*to* **Charmian**)   Darling, this is Stanley Poppin. (*To* **Clifford**.) Charmian!

Clifford   Isn't she? But I saw her first, so hands *off*!

Peter   Yes, we must be off, too.

Clifford   Nice to see you, David.

Peter   Nice to meet you, Stanley. Take care.

Clifford   And if we can't we'll name it after you!

Clifford *takes one of* **Charmian***'s arms,* **Peter** *the other, to lead her off in different direction, as the party noise resumes, and the conversation becomes inaudible again.*

Clifford   [What?]

Peter   [What?]

Clifford   [What are you doing?]

Peter   [What's happening?]

Charmian   [What *is* all this? What's going on?]

Clifford   [Do you mind?]

He takes **Peter***'s hand off* **Charmian***'s arm.* **Clifford** *pulls*
Charmian *away from him.* **Peter** *pushes him aside. They begin to*
struggle. **Charmian** *tries to intervene. The two men pull her out of the way*
in different directions.

Over the noise of the party conversation there can just be distinguished the
sound of huge cosmic laughter. The three of them look upwards as they brawl.

Curtain.

Glassnost

Darkness. Hubbub of audience.

Voice Over PA   Your Majesty . . .

The hubbub dies away.

Your Royal Highness . . . Your Excellencies . . .

The lights come up on a lectern with microphones.

My Lords, Ladies, and Gentlemen . . . Pray silence for the Right
Honourable the Baroness Armament KO GBH RSVP.

Enter, sincerely and energetically, the **Right Honourable the
Baroness Armament KO GBH RSVP**. *Tumultuous applause, off.*

Armament   This is a momentous occasion. As I stand here
before you today . . . at this very special moment in our history
. . . I say this to you . . . and I say it to all of you . . . to all of
you present . . . to all the millions watching at home, live on
television, around the world . . . I say: Look into my eyes, as I
look into yours. Look into my heart, as I look into your hearts.
And if you have an advance press release of the speech you can
tear it up, because here I am departing from my prepared text.
Instead I want to share my thoughts with you today on an aspect
of public life which is all too easily overlooked.

This. These two pieces of glass.

You may not even have noticed them. They are designed to be
inconspicuous. You may not have realised that when I look
sincerely into your eyes like this . . . I am in fact gazing not at
you but at a vision. What is it a vision of? It is a vision of
something of vital importance to all of us. It is a vision of the
words I am about to speak.

Thanks to these two pieces of glass, my words unroll before me in
a manner . . . and I say this to you today in all humility . . . in a
manner remarkably like divine inspiration. And yet they also do
exactly as they're told, like well-trained civil servants. When I

pause to consider ... the words pause to consider. When I race ahead, fired by own eloquence, my thoughts still white-hot from the blazing furnace in my brain, the words tumble over themselves to keep in front of me.

How is this measured supply of words – this precise balance of supply and demand – how is it maintained?

I will be quite frank with you. It is maintained by an underpaid operative concealed in the wings. It is maintained by a gentleman called Kevin Stoop.

Now, let me say this to you today. I am completely dependent upon that wretched underpaid operative. My future, in every sense, is in Kevin Stoop's hands. The only words I have to put before you are the words that he puts before me.

If he had made a mistake, and loaded the machine up with yesterday's speech on regionalisation in the watercress industry, or tomorrow's speech on religious education in army catering schools ... then that is what I should be talking to you about right now. Then again, if he has taken it into his head to replace the speech provided for today, the speech we rehearsed together so recently ... If he has taken it into his head, at the last minute, during the tea break after the rehearsal, to replace that speech with a few thoughts of his own ... then those thoughts of his own are the thoughts which I in all sincerity now find myself sharing with you.

There are certain liberties that we all cherish. If I don't like what I'm saying then I am free, I am perfectly free, to stop saying it ... But until I have said all the words in front of me I will get no more words to say. Kevin Stoop will see to that. The scroll from heaven will cease to unscroll. Silence will fall.

Pause.

And will continue.

Pause.

Until I have uttered every single word. And performed every single stage direction.

Pause. She waggles her fingers in her ears.

What is at issue here is a matter of simple right and wrong.
During that fateful rehearsal beforehand I took it into my head to
scream abuse at Kevin Stoop. I went further. I discharged him
from my employment. Yes, poor abused, long-suffering Kevin
Stoop, who has stuck with me through thick and thin, who has
devoted the best years of his life to keeping my words in front of
me! Simply because I was left speechless for a fraction of a second
while his attention was distracted – distracted by an urgent call on
his mobile from his elderly aunt in Hove! Simply because of this,
I shouted like a lunatic and gave him a week's notice!

There must surely be … I say this quite openly … there must
surely be forever a question over the political judgment of
someone who gives her Autocue operator a week's notice just
before a major speech.

But what I cannot accept, what surely none of us can accept, is
the sheer injustice of it! Not once in all the time he has worked
for me has he abused the absolute trust I have placed in him. He
has kept one step in front of me as faithfully as a horse in front of
a cart. He has given me time to blink regularly, in a lifelike way.
He has paused to let me smile where it says [Smile] …

She smiles.

… and wipe away a tear where it says [Wipe away a tear].

She wipes away a tear.

Sometimes, it's true, he has slowed down just a little in places, to
force me to lay special emphasis on certain particularly important
causes, such as the encouragement of model railways. Or speeded
up just a touch to reduce the impact of all the absolute nonsense I
have spouted over the years about economic policy. But in general
he has been right behind me. Or rather he has been right in front
of me, and I have been right behind him.

How destructive, how terribly destructive, any failure of that
mutual trust can be! Without it I may find myself beginning to go
faster, then faster still, faster and faster, until I am gabbling like a
lunatic and gazing at you with a mad unblinking stare and my

eyeballs wobbling from side to side like ping-pong balls. Then suddenly I . . .

Pause.

Pause . . .

Pause.

And pause . . . The words . . . come one by one . . . For long periods I gaze silently into your eyes . . . You gaze into mine . . . Nothing is said . . . Perhaps we are falling in love, you and I. Perhaps we are going to end up in the *News of the World* together.

And if he suddenly chooses to jump it backwards . . . And if he suddenly chooses to jump it backwards . . . then you'll hear the same thing twice over . . . then you'll hear the same thing twice over . . . But I give you this undertaking: it will be every bit as sincere the second time around. Every bit as sincere the second time around.

So here is what I pledge today: to improve job security for workers in the electronic prompter industry. I give you my solemn word . . . no, I will go further – I give you *his* solemn word . . . to offer all workers in the industry, from today, retrospectively, guaranteed employment for life; to grant them the freedom to fast-forward through anything they find repugnant to their conscience or alien to their interests; and to give them the parking rights which some of them have been so long denied.

Trust me to lead you through the difficult days that lie ahead. Remember: one step in front of me will always be Kevin Stoop!

Curtain.

Toasters

Spott, Much *and* **Candle**. *They are standing, and have been standing for some time. Each is holding, as best he or she can, a plate, a knife and fork, a napkin, a wine glass and a folder of papers. The folders are full; the plates are empty. So are two of the glasses.*

Speaker *(off)* ... and I believe, moreover, that we can look back with some satisfaction upon a period that was marked by its considerable achievements as well as by its inevitable disappointments, a period that will be remembered as a time of searching and of sometimes finding, of striving and of sometimes prevailing; of progress, yes, but also of consolidation; of expansion but also of retrenchment.

Spott *discreetly suppresses a yawn as the speech proceeds.* **Much** *discreetly finishes up the last of his wine.* **Spott** *and* **Candle** *discover that their glasses are empty.* **Spott** *spies a bottle with a little wine in it on the other side of* **Candle***. She discreetly draws* **Candle***'s attention to it.* **Candle** *discreetly contrives to get hold of it, whereupon the others discreetly hold out their glasses to be refilled.* **Candle** *is now holding one more object than it is humanly possible to hold. As she pours, the folder of papers slips away from her, to be fielded by* **Much***, who now in his turn has one more object than etc.* **Much***'s knife and fork are fielded by* **Spott***, who now has etc.*

Speaker I must, I think, here sound a note of caution. When we turn from the recent past to the immediate and longer-term future, we are looking at a projected shortfall, as against previous estimates, of something in the order of three to four per cent on the unadjusted figures, *provided*, and I cannot stress this sufficiently, *provided* there is no corresponding fall-away in the overall uplift, which, in real terms, constitutes scarcely more than standstill funding at a time when the underlying upward trend has been more than offset by a combination of declining returns and returning declines. Suffice it to say that we shall be monitoring results in this area very carefully, and that swift corrective measures will be implemented if need be to keep short-term fluctuations within the parameters established before the present downturn in on-going upswing. But, that being said, perhaps we should try to end on a more positive note. If you would turn for one moment to the papers you have in your folder . . .

Pause. Aghast at this unexpected demand, they attempt to juggle their folders open.

. . . you will see that the figures there have a significant and not unencouraging story to tell. It is all the more gratifying, I think, in view of the prevailing climate of uncertainty, to find, turning for a moment to page 3 . . . page 3 . . .

They struggle to turn to page 3.

. . . that underlying performance for the current period has been so relatively unaffected, if due allowance is made for changes in the way in which data are recorded, changes that are fully explained in the notes at the bottom of page 29 . . . Some further allowance must also be made for the inevitable unforeseen factors, if you would turn for a moment to page 37 . . . Does everyone have page 37 . . . ? You will note in the righthand column a further adjustment for certain non-recurring eventualities such as changes in cut-off levels, to be found in the table on page 15 . . . And on page 22 in the *pink* pages . . . the *pink* pages . . . a once-only provision for assets written off or written down since the previous valuation. In fact the year-on-year figures, turning back to page 3 . . . and I commend them to your particular attention . . . This is page 3 . . . page 3 . . . in the *white* pages . . . On page 51 of which, incidentally, you will find a most important date, and I would ask you to make a note of it in your diaries *now* . . . Thank you. Turning once again to page 3 . . . you will see that the all-important global interim figures show a slight but perceptible rise in percentage terms, and in the current climate that is a result on which I think all concerned must be congratulated . . .

Pause. The sound of uncertain applause. **Spott**, **Much** *and* **Candle** *struggle to join in, tucking glasses under arms, or putting them down on the floor.*

Now will you all make sure your glasses are charged . . .

They snatch up their glasses and discover first that they are empty, then that the bottle is empty as well.

I want to propose a toast to the person who more than anyone else made this remarkable achievement possible. You can probably guess who I'm referring to when I say that this person is a member of a team all of whom have consistently achieved above-average results in office economy, and one of whom, Richard Food, has succeeded in being named twice running as runner-up in the monthly organisational motivation competition . . .

They raise their glasses, concealing their emptiness.

. . . which I think in itself deserves a round of applause.

Applause. **Spott, Much** *and* **Candle** *hurriedly struggle to put their glasses down, or on the floor, in order to join in.*

So would you please raise your glasses . . .

They make haste to recover their glasses and raise them.

. . . and drink a toast to someone who has already enabled this organisation to win a regional efficiency award . . .

Pause. Uncertain applause. **Spott, Much** *and* **Candle** *hurriedly struggle to free their hands again.*

. . . a particularly splendid piece of news . . .

They pick up their glasses.

. . . because it led to our going forward to the national semi-finals . . .

Pause. They bend to put their glasses down and raise their hands to applaud.

Jane Dumble!

They hastily snatch their glasses up again.

Everyone   Jane Dumble!

They drink the toast. Applause. They put their glasses down to join in.

Speaker   Also Jane Dumble's loyal assistant, James Trodden!

Glasses up.

Everyone   James Trodden!

Applause. Glasses down and join in.

Speaker   And while we're drinking toasts I'd like to propose one to Jane's mother, whose fifty-seventh birthday falls I gather exactly one week from today.

Glasses up.

But I know that first Jane and her mother would wish me to mention the rehabilitation centre that has made this anniversary possible . . .

Applause. Glasses down.

But that having been said . . .

Glasses up.

. . . we should spare a thought for rehabilitation centres of every sort that do such magnificent work up and down the country . . .

Applause. Glasses down.

Jane's mother!

Glasses up.

Everyone   Jane's mother!

They drink the toast, then start to put their glasses down.

Speaker   Which brings me by the most natural progression to someone else whose birthday falls this month – Lord Overdrive himself.

They stop, halfway down, hesitating between glasses down and glasses up.

Lord Overdrive's achievements and services have been so many and so various that I have to ask myself where to begin. Should we rather drink to his health . . . ? Or applaud his success . . . ? Raise our glasses to the continuation of his success in the future . . . ? Or show him our appreciation in the usual way . . . ? Perhaps it would be most appropriate for us simply to say . . .

Pause. They hover between air and earth.

. . . Well done!

Spott *applauds.* **Much** *and* **Candle** *drink a toast.*

Much *and* **Candle** (*mumble*)   Well done!

Spott, *seeing* **Much** *and* **Candle** *drink the toast, hastily snatches up her glass and drinks the toast as well – just as* **Much** *and* **Candle**, *seeing* **Spott** *applaud, hastily put their glasses down and applaud.*

Speaker   Let us pray . . .

Spott *drops to her knees.*

Speaker   . . . that we go forward together henceforth . . .

Much, *seeing* **Spott**, *drops to his knees as well, just as* **Candle** *hauls* **Spott** *to her feet again . . .*

Speaker   . . . to achieve further no less encouraging results. One final point: I realise what a burden has fallen on everyone here today. I know how full everyone's hands have been. So let's end by giving a very special tribute to ourselves. Let's show the world just what we can do, by raising our glasses . . .

They raise their glasses.

. . . and clapping *at the same time.*

They applaud at the same time. A huge sound of chinking and smashing glass. Everything finally slips away from **Much**, **Spott** *and* **Candle**, *and goes everywhere. They suck glass out of fingers, put napkins to severed wrists, etc.*

Curtain.

Immobiles

Darkness. The ringing of a phone.

Lights up on the phone, centre, with an answering machine beside it. The ringing ceases and the answering machine answers.

Chris's voice *Hi! Chris and Nikki aren't here right now, so why don't you wait for the funny little noise, then leave them a funny little message?*

Beep.

Lights up on **Dietrich***, left. He is standing by a coin-box (phone 2 – the first of eleven coin-boxes that will appear in various parts of the set) holding the receiver, a suitcase at his feet.*

Lights down on the answering machine.

Dietrich Hello, yes – Chris and Nikki! It's me, Dietrich. I am so looking forward to seeing you both again! It is so kind of you to come and meet me at the airport – most unnecessary, but a very nice welcome, so thank you – and, well, here I am! At the airport! So, I look forward to seeing you . . . I gave you the right date, yes, the fifteenth? And the time, 1840 . . . ? So, no hurry – I wait for you here . . . I like very much your humorous message, by the way.

Lights down on **Dietrich***. Lights up on* **Chris***. He is standing by another coin-box right (phone 3), holding the receiver. He waits, listening to the dialling tone: brr brr, brr brr.*

Chris's voice *Hi! Chris and Nikki aren't here right now, so why don't you wait for the funny little noise, then leave them a funny little message?*

Beep.

Chris Oh, God, that message is a mistake – I must change it . . . It's me, Chris, I'm at the airport. No sign of Dietrich, though. There *wasn't* a flight from Düsseldorf at 1840 . . . I just wondered if he'd rung or anything . . . Only you're not there for some reason . . . Where are you . . . ? No Dietrich, no you, just me, standing at Arrivals in Terminal One . . . You did say

Terminal One . . . ? I hope this is not the start of one of those terrible sagas . . . There's a flight at 1920, at Terminal *Two*. I'd better go and have a look at that. If he rings, tell him I'll be at Terminal Two. *Two*, yes . . . ?

Lights down on **Chris**. *Lights up on Dietrich at phone 2. He waits, receiver to ear, as before.*

Dialling tone: brr brr, brr brr.

Chris's voice   *Hi! Chris and Nikki aren't here right now, so why don't you wait for the funny little noise, then leave them a funny little message?*

Beep.

Dietrich   Hello, Chris and Nikki! It's Dietrich again. I like your humorous message even more the second time I hear it . . . I'm sorry to be such a pest, but I don't know should I wait here at the airport or not . . . I can easily come to your house . . . Only, if you are on your way . . . Bad traffic, perhaps . . . So kind of you . . . I wait here one more hour maybe, and then . . . I don't know . . . I look forward to see you.

Lights down on **Dietrich**. *Lights up on* **Nikki** *at the answering machine, listening.*

Dietrich's voice   *. . . Bad traffic, perhaps . . . So kind of you . . . I wait here one more hour maybe, and then . . . I don't know . . . I look forward to see you.*

Long beep.

Nikki *presses Record on the answering machine.*

Nikki   Hello, Dietrich, this is a message for Dietrich, from Nikki, in case you ring again. Dietrich, Chris is there, at the airport, there's a message from him on the machine, he missed you somehow, and now he's gone to Terminal Two. Two, OK? I've got to go out again – shop for supper. Sorry to talk so fast, but you have to fit the outgoing message into . . .

Beep.

. . . the space, and it's run out already.

She presses Record again. Lights down on **Nikki**. *Lights up on* **Dietrich** *at phone 2.*

Nikki's voice   . . . *and now he's gone to Terminal Two. Two, OK? I've got to go out again – shop for supper. Sorry to talk so fast, but you have to fit the outgoing message into . . .*

Beep.

Dietrich   Hello, Nikki, it's Dietrich again. Well, so – we make contact at last! I heard your message, yes, very good, very clear, thank you, I like it even more than your humorous message. So kind of you. And yes, I will go to Terminal Two. If Chris rings again, tell him to wait there, at Terminal Two. So kind of him to meet me. So sorry to be such a pain in the behind.

Lights down on **Dietrich**. *Lights up on* **Chris** *at phone 3. He listens patiently.*

Nikki's voice   . . . *and now he's gone to Terminal Two. Two, OK? I've got to go out again – shop for supper. Sorry to talk so fast, but you have to fit the outgoing message into . . .*

Beep.

Chris   Yes, well, it's not Dietrich, it's me. So – Dietrich is floating around Heathrow somewhere? Where exactly, of course, you don't bother to say. Not at at Terminal *Two*, evidently, because I was *at* Terminal Two. Now I'm back at Terminal *One*. But if he gets your message then he *will* go to Terminal Two . . . All right, I'll go to Terminal Two again . . . I sometimes seriously wonder if life is worth living . . . And where are *you*? I thought your mother was coming today, I thought you were waiting in for your mother – I thought that was why *I* was meeting Dietrich . . . ? Right – Terminal Two. If he rings again tell him to stay at Terminal Two . . . Maddening – he's your chum, not mine . . .

Lights down on **Chris**. *Lights up on* **Dietrich** *at phone 2.*

Nikki's voice   . . . *and now he's gone to Terminal Two. Two, OK? I've got to go out again – shop for supper. Sorry to talk so fast, but you have to fit the outgoing message into . . .*

Beep.

Dietrich   Hello, Nikki, this is Dietrich. Now things go from bad to worse – I cannot find Terminal Two! There is no Terminal Two at Gatwick! Nikki, do you mean the North Terminal . . . ? Maybe you mean the North Terminal . . . I think I go to the North Terminal . . . So kind of you to take all this trouble . . .

Lights down on **Dietrich***. Lights up on* **Chris***, at phone 4. He listens with eyes closed.*

Nikki's voice   *. . . and now he's gone to Terminal Two. Two, OK? I've got to go out again – shop for supper. Sorry to talk so fast, but you have to fit the outgoing message into . . .*

Beep.

Chris   If I have to listen to that message once more I'll scream – it's even more maddening than the last one . . . I'm at Terminal Two, and of course there's no sign of the bloody man . . . He might be anywhere! Terminal Three, Terminal Four, the bar, the restaurant, the lavatory . . . Unless you said *Gatwick*. You didn't say Gatwick, did you, by any chance . . . ? You said *don't* go somewhere, I remember that . . . Did you say don't go to Gatwick? Or don't go to Heathrow? *Asinine* thing to say – *don't* go somewhere . . .

Lights down on **Chris***, still speaking. Lights up on* **Nikki** *at the answering machine. She tries to control her irritation.*

Chris's voice   *. . . Did you say don't go to Gatwick? Or don't go to Heathrow?* Asinine *thing to say –* don't *go somewhere . . . But since you're still floating around God knows where there's no way of finding out . . . I can't drive to Gatwick now . . . I suppose he may have gone back to Terminal One . . . I'll try Terminal One again, for the last time, because then I'm coming home . . .*

Long beep.

She presses Record.

Nikki   Dietrich, so sorry, my idiot husband has gone to Heathrow, I told him Gatwick, and he went to Heathrow . . . ! Don't you listen to a single word I say? Not Dietrich – you! Dietrich, get on the train, there's a train, it goes to Victoria, come to Victoria, I'll jump in the car and meet you at Victoria. Victoria

Station. So sorry – we're both longing to . . .

Beep.

. . . see you, only now I'm talking to myself again!

She punches Record. Lights down on **Nikki***. Lights up on* **Dietrich** *at phone 2.*

Nikki's voice   . . . *Victoria, I'll jump in the car and meet you at Victoria. Victoria Station. So sorry – we're both longing to . . .*

Beep.

Dietrich   Nikki, this is Dietrich. Thank you, yes, I've got your message. I like also this message, by the way! So, I will take the train – that was my original idea, you know, before you kindly said you would meet me – and I will meet you at Victoria. Most unnecessary, but most nice of you . . . Oh, Nikki, I'm so sorry to cause you all this trouble. So sorry about poor Chris going to Heathrow. Maybe my English was not quite clear . . . But now this time – no mistake . . . Victoria, yes? Not Waterloo, not King's Cross – Victoria! Anyway, thank you for a new experience – it was quite interesting for me to see the North Terminal . . . Oh, what am I thinking of? – You won't get this message – you're already on your way to Victoria!

Lights down on **Nikki***. Lights up on* **Chris***, at phone 3. He listens, rigid with irritation.*

Nikki's voice   *Dietrich, so sorry, my idiot husband has gone to Heathrow, I told him Gatwick, and he went to Heathrow . . . ! Don't you listen to a single word I say? Not Dietrich – you. Dietrich, get on the train, there's a train, it goes to Victoria, come to Victoria, I'll jump in the car and meet you at Victoria. Victoria Station. So sorry – we're both longing to . . .*

Beep.

Chris   Thank you for your charming message. If I sometimes don't hear what you say at breakfast then it's because you say it while I'm reading the newspaper, something I've warned you about a million times, but I won't labour it again now, firstly because this morning I *did* hear you – you said 'Don't go to Gatwick.' Or 'Don't go to Heathrow.' Or something equally

misleading. Secondly because this is my last coin, and the phone's
going to run out at any moment, and thirdly because you're not
there to hear it, since you're driving to Victoria to meet your
chum, or rather, *not* driving to Victoria, but walking hopelessly up
and down the street outside the house looking for the car, then
slowly remembering that the car's at Heathrow with me. And
there's a fourth, rather more important reason why I can't hang
around here phoning you from Terminal One at Heathrow,
delightful as it is – because you seem to have forgotten that . . .

*Dialling tone. He takes the receiver away from his ear and gazes at it. Lights
down on* **Chris**. *Lights up on* **Nikki**, *entering centre. She rushes to the
answering machine and punches Record.*

Nikki   No! CAN'T meet you at Victoria! No car – car at
Heathrow with idiot husband! DON'T WAIT, GET A TAXI . . . !
Hold on – no – you won't get this message – you're on the train
– I'll have to come on the tube – only now I'm going to be
late . . . WAIT AT VICTORIA . . . ! Oh, and Chris, you
WEREN'T reading the paper when I told you, you were looking
straight at me, so I thought . . .

Beep.

. . . you might be taking something in for once, but you weren't,
any more than this bloody machine is, because nobody in the
world seems to be listening to anything any more!

She punches Record, and runs out centre. Lights down on **Nikki**. *Lights up
on* **Chris**, *at phone 3.*

Nikki's voice   . . . *WAIT AT VICTORIA . . . ! Oh, and, Chris, you
WEREN'T reading the paper when I told you, you were looking straight at
me, so I thought . . .*

Beep.

Chris (*calmly*)   Yes, as I was saying, before the money ran out,
and I had to go to the shop and buy myself a telephone card,
because they wouldn't give me any change for the phone unless I
bought something, so I bought a phonecard for one pound, and
I'd only got a twenty-pound note, and they only had small
change, so now I've got a phonecard *and* nineteen pounds in loose

change, which means that I can now stand here, with my trousers sagging a little under the weight of the coins, and talk to our answering machine for the rest of the night, except that I can't, because you've obviously forgotten, in all your excitement about meeting your lovely chum, about your mother arriving – something *I* reminded *you* about at breakfast, only you obviously weren't listening, even though you weren't reading the paper, even though I'd carefully got your attention before I began to speak – so I've got to come screaming back up the motorway to let her in, though by the time I get there, even as it is, she's likely to have been standing outside in the rain for some considerable time. Though of course if you've got this message you'll have got back and found her there yourself . . .

Lights down on **Chris**. *Lights up on* **Mother**, *at phone 5, receiver to ear. She listens, puzzled, hand over her other ear.*

Nikki's voice   *No! CAN'T meet you at Victoria! No car – car at Heathrow with idiot husband! DON'T WAIT, GET A TAXI . . . ! Hold on – no – you won't get this message – you're on the train – I'll have to come on the tube – only now I'm going to be late . . . WAIT AT VICTORIA . . . ! Oh, and Chris, you WEREN'T reading the paper when I told you, you were looking straight at me, so I thought . . .*

Beep.

Mother   Nicola, darling, it's Mummy. Oh dear, I hope everything's all right . . . I can't quite understand what you're saying about Victoria – the noise here is simply frightful. I'm not at Victoria, darling – why do you think I'm at Victoria? I'm in a public house called the Bag O'Nails, just round the corner from you – I couldn't find a phone anywhere else . . . I can't think for the noise . . . Can you hear what I'm saying . . . ? I rang your bell . . . I'm not quite sure what's happening . . . I looked through the letter-box, and I thought I could hear Christopher's voice . . . Perhaps you're having some sort of . . . little talk about things together. If so I'll wait here, of course . . . There are some quite strange people in here – Care in the community, I suppose. Nicola, darling, I do find it odd that you should want to live in a neighbourhood like this . . . though of course it's nothing to do with me. I'll try to wait here until . . . well, until.

Lights down on **Mother**. *Lights up on* **Nikki**, *at phone 6, receiver to ear. She listens impatiently.*

Nikki's voice   ... *WAIT AT VICTORIA* ...*! Oh, and Chris, you WEREN'T reading the paper when I told you, you were looking straight at me, so I thought* ...

Beep.

Nikki   Oh God, I thought you'd be back by now ... I'm at the tube – I was on my way to Victoria to meet Dietrich – only I suddenly remembered Mummy's arriving ... You'll have to let her in ... Only you're not there, of course ... Oh no! She must be on the doorstep ... ! I'll have to come back – *you'll* have to go to Victoria. He's going to be waiting at Victoria ... He's not *my* friend. I don't know why you say he's *my* friend. You hate it when I call people *your* friends instead of *our* friends ... Wait for Mummy first, if she's not there, then go to Victoria ... No, don't wait for Mummy, I'll deal with Mummy, don't do anything complicated – just GO TO VICTORIA!

Lights down on **Nikki**. *Lights up on* **Chris** *at the answering machine.*

Nikki's voice   ... *No, don't wait for Mummy, I'll deal with Mummy, don't do anything complicated – just GO TO VICTORIA!*

Long beep.

He presses Record.

Chris   No, your mother's not on the doorstep. I've just got back and found a message from her saying she's in a particularly sordid and notorious local pub. So I will go and fetch her out of it before she's murdered by drug-dealers. Nikki, you go to Victoria. Mother and Dietrich – you both stay EXACTLY WHERE YOU ARE!

Beep. He presses Record. Lights down on **Chris**. *Lights up on* **Dietrich** *at phone 7.*

Chris's voice   ... *Nikki, you go to Victoria. Mother and Dietrich – you both stay EXACTLY WHERE YOU ARE!*

Beep.

Dietrich   Well, here I am at Victoria. And yes, of course, thank you, I wait here, exactly where I am . . . Only that sounds bad about Nikki's mother and the drug-dealers . . . I'm so sorry . . . I'm afraid I'm causing you a big disruption. Well, I wait here . . .

Lights down on **Dietrich**. *Lights up on* **Chris** *at phone 5.*

Chris's voice   . . . *both stay EXACTLY WHERE YOU ARE!*

Beep.

Chris   Right, I'm at the pub. Only of course your mother isn't here. I asked someone at the bar if they'd seen anyone who looked like your mother, and he offered me a snort of cocaine . . . Now what . . . ? Perhaps just give up . . . Give up on everything, toot the coke . . .

Lights down on **Chris**. *Lights up on* **Nikki** *at the answering machine.*

Chris's voice   . . . *Perhaps just give up . . . Give up on everything, toot the coke . . .*

Long beep.

Nikki *punches Record.*

Beep.

Nikki   Chris, I'm back – stay at the pub . . . Which pub, incidentally? Why don't you say which pub? Anyway, I'll search the streets, in case . . . Dietrich – so sorry, you must think we're all going totally crazy . . .

She punches Record.

Beep.

Lights down on **Nikki**. *Lights up on* **Mother** *at phone 8.*

Nikki's voice   . . . *Anyway, I'll search the streets, in case . . . Dietrich – so sorry, you must think we're all going totally crazy . . .*

Beep.

Mother   Nicola, darling, it's Mummy again. Oh, dear, I'm very sorry – I'm in a kind of restaurant in the High Street. It's called Spud-U-Like. I didn't want you coming into that terrible public house ... But Chris is there, is he? I'd better go back there. Don't worry. I'll be all right in there – I've got my umbrella.

Lights down on **Mother**. *Lights up on the answering machine.*

Nikki's voice   ... *Anyway, I'll search the streets, in case* ... *Dietrich – so sorry, you must think we're all going totally crazy* ...

Beep.

Lights down on answering machine, up on **Chris**, *at phone 8.*

Chris   Oh, so now you're out wandering the streeets? I told you to stay where you were! Why don't you EVER LISTEN TO WHAT I SAY ... ? I've now wasted the entire evening struggling to locate your friends and relations ... I've looked in every single café and bar along the High Street. I'm now in Spud-U-Like ... I'll try the house again ...

Lights down on **Chris**, *up on the answering machine.*

Nikki's voice   ... *Anyway, I'll search the streets, in case* ... *Dietrich – so sorry, you must think we're all going totally crazy* ...

Beep.

Lights down on the answering machine, up on **Nikki**, *at phone 8.*

Nikki   I suppose you're still in the pub ... Wherever it is ... I've looked in all the cafés and bars along the High Street ... I'm in Spud-U-Like ... I'll go back to the house ...

Lights down on **Nikki**. *Lights up on* **Dietrich** *at phone 5, suitcase at his feet, hand to ear.*

Nikki's voice   ... *Dietrich – so sorry, you must think we're all going totally crazy* ...

Beep.

Dietrich   It's Dietrich again, I'm afraid. Can you hear this? I am calling from a rather noisy place. So, well, I waited at Victoria for some time, not very long, an hour perhaps, but clearly I have not understood quite right, so I took a taxi, and I came to your house ... I thought I hear voices inside, but no one answers the bell ... It's raining, so I am waiting in a pub called the Bag

O'Nails, which is an amusing name, but I think I must go soon, there is a somewhat bad atmosphere here . . .

Lights down on **Dietrich**. *Lights up on* **Nikki** *at phone 9.*

Nikki's voice   . . . *Dietrich – so sorry, you must think we're all going totally crazy* . . .

Beep.

Nikki   She's not at the house . . . I'm so worried . . . I'm at the phones in front of the police station . . . They haven't had any reports of her . . . I'll try all the pubs again . . .

Lights down on **Nikki**, *up on the answering machine.*

Nikki's voice   . . . *Dietrich – so sorry, you must think we're all going totally crazy* . . .

Lights up on **Chris** *at phone 9. Lights down on answering machine.*

Beep.

Chris   You're *still* not back! Nikki, what the hell are you playing at . . . ? Listen, I'm at the phones in front of the police station – I'm going to report your mother missing . . .

Lights down on **Chris**. *Lights up on* **Dietrich** *at phone 10, bandaged, minus suitcase.*

Nikki's voice   . . . *we're all going totally crazy* . . .

Beep.

Dietrich   Hello, it's Dietrich . . . Dietrich . . . I can't talk very clear . . . There is a problem with my jaw . . . My jaw . . . Not to worry, everyone is very kind, I am at the Royal Infirmary. All my fault, I'm afraid. They say I should have rolled up like a ball and covered my head. But I have to ask another favour, because I regret to say I lost sight of my suitcase while I was unconscious . . . Or maybe I can buy a toothbrush here . . .

He puts his hand in his pocket.

Wait – I call you back . . .

Dietrich *hangs up and remains at the phone, feeling all his pockets.*

Lights up on **Mother** *at phone 11.*

Nikki's voice   *... we're all going totally crazy ...*

Beep.

Mother   Nicola, darling, I'm at the police station. Now, don't worry, darling, they arrested me in that public house, it's quite ludicrous – how you can live in a neighbourhood like this ... Anyway, they're charging me with assault, and it's all very ridiculous – I was simply trying to stop these people kicking this nice German gentleman, but if you could possibly come here and arrange bail ... I think I'll try to hold on until you come in, because they only let you make one call ...

Mother *remains at the phone. Lights up on* **Chris** *at phone 5, receiver to one ear, hand to other.*

Chris (*shouts*)   Is that you?

Call waiting   Please hold the line while we try to connect you.

Chris   Listen, I'm back in the Bag O'Nails ...

Call waiting   The number you are calling knows you are waiting.

Chris   I can't hear a word you're saying – it's getting more hellish in here by the moment ...

Lights up on **Nikki** *at phone 12, just behind* **Chris**'s *back, elbowing him as she furiously dials.*

Call Waiting   Please hold the line while we try to connect you.

Chris (*shouts*)   What?

Call waiting   The number you are calling knows you are waiting.

Chris   You'll have to shout ...

Call waiting   Please try later.

Chris (*understands*)   Oh, no!

He slams the receiver down and stands roaring with frustration. **Dietrich** *dials, at phone 10 still.*

Nikki (*shouts*)   Listen, I'm in a dreadful pub called the Bag O'Nails . . .

Call waiting   Please hold the line while we try to connect you.

Nikki   What? There's some drunken lunatic shouting in my ear . . .

Call waiting   The number you are calling knows you are waiting.

Nikki   *Who's* waiting?

Call waiting   Please hold the line while we try to connect you.

Nikki *screams and slams the receiver down. She and* **Chris** *both feverishly redial.*

Mother   Hello? I'm not sure how much longer they'll let me hold on . . .

Dietrich   Hello?

Call waiting   Please hold the line while we try to connect you.

Dietrich   Yes, because now sadly in the hospital also my wallet has gone astray . . .

Now everyone speaks or shouts at once, together with the engaged signal, as electronic noises come up and the lights go down.

Chris   Will you put the phone down, you stupid woman, and listen to what I'm saying? You've been yattering away for the past hour . . .

Nikki   Will you shut up, whoever you are, and put the phone down, and listen to what I'm saying, before I go completely out of my mind . . . ?

Call waiting   The number you are calling knows you are waiting . . . Please hold the line while we try to connect you . . .

Mother   Or I could stay the night here, of course, but then perhaps you could put some overnight things in a bag and bring them round when you have a moment . . .

Dietrich   And I think my passport, yes, and my watch, though fortunately it was not a valuable one, only two or three hundred marks . . .

Curtain.

Printed in the USA
CPSIA information can be obtained
at www.ICGtesting.com
LVHW041057171024
794057LV00001B/131